Samuel D. Marshall

Tarantulas and Other Arachnids

Everything About Purchase, Care, Nutrition, Behavior, and Housing

Filled with Full-color Photographs
Illustrations by Laura Barghusen

BARRON'S

2 CONTENTS

**Understanding
Tarantulas**   5

What Are Tarantulas?   5

Where Are Tarantulas
Found?   5

A Bad Reputation   6

Tarantula Anatomy   7

Predators of the Tarantula   11

Lifestyles of the
Big and Hairy   14

Tarantula Defense   15

Tarantula Basics   17

Why Do You Want a
Tarantula?   17

Buying a Tarantula   17

Housing   20

Substrates   22

Cage Types   25

Cage Pests   31

Tarantula Food   34

Diet   34

The Molt   36

HOW-TO: Handling
Your Tarantula   38

**Commonly Available
Species**   41

Understanding Systematics   41

Species Accounts   45

Box: Tarantulas
and the Law   59

Breeding Tarantulas   73

Sex and the Single
Tarantula   73

Getting a Pair   73

Consenting Adults?   76

The Big Night   78

After Mating   79

Rearing Babies 85

Starting Out 85

When to Separate
the Spiderlings 85

Housing Spiderlings 86

Feeding 87

Catching Food and Caring
for Your Sick Tarantula 89

What's for Dinner? 89

Finding Commercial
Sources 89

HOW–TO: Caring for
Your Sick Tarantula 94

Other Arachnids 97

Other Spiders 97

Scorpions 102

Those Weird Spider
Relatives 106

Information 109

Index 110

UNDERSTANDING TARANTULAS

Tarantulas are legendary creatures. In addition to their awesome size and unique hairiness, there is always a mystique attached to tarantulas that evokes in our minds the exotic deserts and jungles of the world.

What Are Tarantulas?

Amazingly, despite their infamy, there is very little known about tarantula biology. The primary reason for the biological obscurity of tarantulas is that few people perform research on the group. Even taxonomy, which is relatively well known for other spiders, is poorly understood because tarantula anatomy is not as variable as that of other spiders, which makes it harder to make rules for identification. In spite of all this, tarantulas are currently among the most popular of the nontraditional pets. Keeping a tarantula gives a window on worlds we did not even dream existed, the vast realm of invertebrate diversity. By keeping and observing one of these beautiful animals, we will learn a little about life among that multitude of other, rarely seen animals.

Tarantulas are in the class Arachnida (which includes ticks, mites, scorpions, harvestmen, and others), order Araneae (all spiders), infraorder Mygalomorphae (which includes trapdoor spiders, purseweb spiders, and others as well as tarantulas), and finally the tarantula family Theraphosidae. In this book, I will use the name tarantula to refer to members of the family Theraphosidae, and no others. (This needs pointing out as some authors refer to all mygalomorph spiders as tarantulas.) Other than sheer size, tarantulas are set apart from the rest of the spiders by having the following combination of characteristics:

1. They breathe using two pair of book lungs (a type of respiratory organ described on page 11);

2. They have fangs that move up and down instead of sideways (like all other spiders); and

3. They have two claws and adhesive pads on each foot.

Where Are Tarantulas Found?

There are about 850 species worldwide. Tarantulas are found in the tropical and subtropical regions of the world. Their range includes Africa and Madagascar, parts of the Middle East, southern Europe, southern Asia, the Indo-Pacific region, Australia, northern

*The stunning lesserblack tarantula (**Xenesthis immanis**) is rarely available because exports from Colombia are currently banned.*

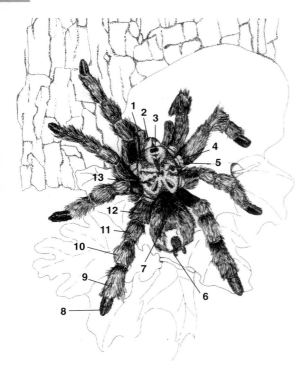

The external anatomy of a tarantula, dorsal (top) view.
1. pedipalp
2. chelicera
3. eyes
4. trochanter
5. coxa
6. spinnerets
7. abdomen
8. tarsus
9. metatarsus
10. tibia
11. patella
12. femur
13. cephalothorax

New Zealand, some of the Micronesian Islands (Ponape, Palau), all of Central and South America, parts of the Caribbean, and the United States north to central California and east to the Mississippi River.

A Bad Reputation

The tarantula's bad reputation began in southern Europe during the Middle Ages with a large burrowing wolf spider *Lycosa tarentula*, which was thought to be dangerously venomous. The name *tarantula* derives from the city of Taranto in northern Italy, and a popular dance, the Tarantella, which was supposed to cure the effects of a tarantula's

bite. It has been proposed that real or imagined tarantula bites were used as an excuse to dance wildly, something the Church frowned upon at the time. The memory of this big, bad wolf spider was brought to the Americas by Europeans, and the name tarantula was quickly applied to a totally different type of spider: spiders in the family Theraphosidae. Perhaps the first recorded use of the name tarantula for these New World spiders is in a narrative by Jonathan Stedman, a British adventurer and mercenary, traveling in Suriname (in northeastern South America) in the 1770s in his *Narrative of a Five Years Expedition*. During his travels Stedman was shown a large hairy spider in a bottle that he described as being dark brown in color and having a leg span of over 8 inches (20.3 cm). Based on his description, this spider was probably the goliath birdeater tarantula *Theraphosa blondi*. Stedman noted that the spider was misnamed "tarantula" by the Surinamese. There is some argument over what popular name to use for theraphosid spi-

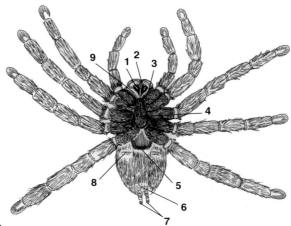

The external anatomy of a tarantula, ventral (bottom) view.
1. chelicera
2. fang
3. labium
4. sternum
5. genital aperture
6. anus
7. spinnerets
8. book lung
9. maxilla

ders. Alternatives include tarantula, birdeating spider, mygale, baboon spider, monkey spider, and on and on. Most of the furor is over the fact that the name tarantula was initially applied to a wolf spider. Wolf spiders are not closely related to the large, hairy theraphosid spiders we now call tarantulas. However, the wolf spider from southern Europe (*Lycosa tarentula*) does look something like a tarantula and digs a burrow like many tarantulas do.

When Europeans started to settle the New World, the name tarantula was already firmly established in the popular mythology of spiders. The first of what are now called tarantulas (the family Theraphosidae) was not brought to the attention of scientists until 1705 when Maria Sibylla Merian, a Swiss naturalist visiting Suriname, included a painting of a large, hairy spider eating a hummingbird in her book on the insects of Suriname. This tarantula was the pinktoe tarantula. In fact, the Latin genus name it was given, *Avicularia*, refers to bird eating (Avi- = bird; -cularia = eating). Her readers in Europe were horrified at the idea that a spider could turn the tables and eat a bird. Merian's picture, as well as one in a book

on Amazonian travels by English naturalist Henry Walter Bates published in 1866 in *A Naturalist on the Rivers Amazon*, depicting a pinktoe tarantula eating a sparrow, led to British naturalists adopting the name birdeating spider and drawing a sharp distinction between these supposed bird eaters and the wolf spiders called tarantulas in Europe. However, this dramatic birdeating behavior is almost certainly rare in the wild. Tarantulas will eat almost anything they can catch and hang onto, but since they are mostly active at night, they will not often come across sparrows or hummingbirds, which are active during the day. For better or worse, the name tarantula is now widely accepted as applying to the big, hairy theraphosids we find so fascinating.

Tarantula Anatomy

Tarantula anatomy is basically the same as that of the small house spider living in a web under your bathroom sink. Spiders are arthropods and have an exoskeleton. This exoskeleton is made up of cuticle, a material that is strong, waterproof, and lightweight. Everything you see when you look at a tarantula is cuticle, even the hairs. These hairs are technically called setae and are projections of the cuticle; they do not grow out of follicles the way mammalian hair does.

All spiders have two main body divisions: the front section, called the cephalothorax (also called the prosoma by some sources), and the rear end, called the abdomen (sometimes referred to as the opisthosoma). These two parts are joined by a narrow waist called a pedicel. Unlike insects (and spiders in some cartoons), spiders have no separate head and neck or antennae. All the main appendages attach to the cephalothorax—the eight legs, the food-handling feet called the pedipalps, and the mouth parts. The mouth parts include the muscular fang bases and the attached backward-pointing fangs, which together form the chelicerae. The tarantula's venom glands are inside the basal part. The first part of the digestive tract and what the tarantula has for a brain are inside the cephalothorax.

On top, near the front, the tarantula has eight little eyes on the ocular tubercle, which is a small, oval, raised area. Despite all these eyes, tarantulas can hardly see at all; they rely almost entirely on touch, taste, and smell to perceive their world. They do not smell using any kind of nose but have organs on their feet for perceiving airborne chemicals and humidity. There are also chemically sensitive hairs on the legs and pedipalps that act as taste organs.

Inside the abdomen are all the rest of the vital organs: the rest of the digestive tract, the heart (a muscular tube that runs the length of the top of the abdomen), the book lungs, the silk-producing organs, and the reproductive organs.

Tarantula blood is very different from the blood of vertebrates (animals with backbones). Tarantula blood is called hemolymph and is a clear, sometimes pale blue or yellow color.

The book lungs are so named because internally they look like the pages of a book. Each lung is a folded area of the cuticle that allows the exchange of oxygen and carbon dioxide between the blood that flows between the "pages" (or lamellae) and the atmosphere on the other side of the thin membrane of each "page." This gas exchange is passive. Tarantulas cannot breathe using any kind of movement of the leaves of the book lung.

The small fingerlike projections from the end of the abdomen are spinnerets, which the spider uses to secrete silk. You can see these wave in the air when the tarantula is walking around. If you look closely you can see the strands of silk that they leave behind them to mark their passage.

Close-up of a female Peruvian blond tarantula (**Lasiodorides polycuspalatus**).

A mating pair of Texas tan tarantulas (**Aphonopelma anax**). *The male is reaching under the female.*

Tarantula Sex

Spider sex has an unusual twist to it as males transfer sperm indirectly using their secondary sexual organs. The primary genital organ for all spiders is on the underside of the abdomen near the front of the body. However, when they mature, male spiders develop uniquely modified pedipalps to transfer the sperm to the female. The last joint of the pedipalps develops into a complicated bulblike structure called the cymbium bearing the bulb and embolus, which function together like a syringe. After they mature, male tarantulas spin a little hammock of silk (called a sperm web), deposit a drop of sperm from their genital aperture onto it, and then dip the business end of the embolus into the drop of sperm and draw it up into the bulb for later use. Tarantulas mate face to face; the male reaches under the female and inserts the embolus into the female's genital aperture. It is fairly easy to spot the modified pedipalps of the males as they are club shaped instead of pointed like one of the feet. Most adult male tarantulas also have tibial spurs on the underside of the first pair of legs at the end of the tibia (there are rare exceptions to this). You will definitely want to be able to recognize adult male tarantulas, as they do not make good pets. One of the main reasons is that, upon maturation, many male tarantulas have only several months to live. In contrast, females can go on to live for many years; there are records of 20 years or more in the case of tarantulas from the American Southwest. It is difficult to sex immature tarantulas without shed skins (see page 36).

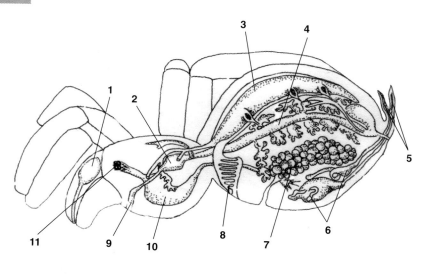

The internal anatomy of a tarantula with the major organ systems.

1. venom gland
2. sucking stomach
3. heart
4. gut
5. spinnerets
6. silk glands
7. ovary
8. book lung
9. esophagus
10. ganglion (what the spider has for a brain)
11. eyes

Digestion

Spiders have external digestion. This means that what they actually swallow is a predigested and highly nutritious soup. They digest their prey by using a combination of venom and digestive juices. Tarantulas also grind up the prey item into a type of meatball and alternatively suck in the digested part and regurgitate more digestive fluids onto the rest. A hungry tarantula can take hours to finish a large prey item but they can do a very thorough job. Less-hungry tarantulas may leave behind leftovers.

Tarantula Ecology

Tarantulas spend their days in silk-lined retreats and hunt by emerging at dusk and sitting (usually half in and half out of the retreat) and waiting for something to pass by. All spiders (and most arachnids) are strict carnivores. The only exceptions are mites, many of which feed on plants, and harvestmen (also called daddylonglegs), which will occasionally scavenge. Most of the wandering done by tarantulas is by mature males in search of mating opportunities. Being such stay-at-homes means that they have to take their prey as it comes, rather than go looking for it.

Longevity

American tarantulas can take up to 10 years to mature (depending on the species and food availability), and, as mentioned above, the females can live for 20 years beyond that. The tropical species have a higher metabolic rate and mature faster, with most species taking two to three years to mature. Tarantulas have evolved a life strategy of patience—waiting for prey, deferring reproduction, and reproducing only once a

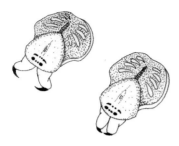

The fangs of most spiders (in the spider sub-order Araneomorphae) articulate from side-to-side. This may give them greater grasping power when they bite prey.

year when they do breed. Tarantula longevity is part of what makes them such good spider pets. Most common spiders measure out their lives in months, not years.

Respiratory Organs

Tarantulas are considered primitive by many arachnologists—sort of spider dinosaurs— because they have anatomic features that are considered old-fashioned by spider biologists. One of these is their respiratory organs. All tarantulas breathe using two pair of book lungs, which are on the underside of the abdomen toward the front of the spider. Most common spiders use tracheae in addition to one pair of book lungs. Tracheae are tubes that lead from the outside deep into the body. The problem with book lungs (compared with tracheae) is that they lose a lot of water due to evaporation. This causes problems for tarantulas because, like

Tarantula fangs articulate vertically, rather than from side-to-side. This is a characteristic of the spider sub-order Mygalomorphae.

all spiders, tarantulas extend their legs using blood pressure rather than muscles and losing water from the body lowers the tarantula's blood pressure. What can then happen is that even a mildly thirsty tarantula may not be able to walk if it does not get a drink.

Fangs

Another tarantula feature that is considered "old-fashioned" is the way that the fangs attach to the body. All spiders in the spider infraorder Mygalomorphae (which includes tarantulas) have fangs that move up and down. In contrast, the more modern spiders' fangs move from side to side, which means that they act like pincers when grabbing prey. Tarantula fangs do not close on anything but are used to stab and pull the prey against the body. This is thought to be less efficient as tarantulas cannot grab prey as easily or safely as other spiders.

Predators of the Tarantula

Tarantulas may seem to be big and nasty enough that nothing in the deserts or jungles where they live would want to mess with them. However, their large size makes a nice meal for

A giant pompillid wasp that specializes in hunting and parasitizing the giant goliath birdeater tarantula.

A pinktoe tarantula (Avicularia avicularia) sits in her retreat in a curled banana leaf.

A close-up of an adult male Chilean common tarantula (Grammostola rosea).

An adult female skeleton tarantula (Ephebopus murinus).

An adult female Chilean common tarantula (Grammostola rosea).

An adult male skeleton tarantula (Ephebopus murinus).

An adult female Peruvian blond tarantula (Lasiodorides polycuspulatus).

Adult female Costa Rican tigerrump tarantula (Cyclosternum fasciatum)— one of the most beautiful of all tarantulas.

many kinds of predator. The coatimundi (*Nasua* spp., a tropical relative of the raccoon) is known to be an avid predator of tarantulas in parts of its range. One of the most dangerous enemies are wasps in the family Pompilidae (*Pepsis* sp.), which specializes in hunting tarantulas. The female wasp paralyzes the tarantula with a sting and then often stashes the stunned but living tarantula's body in the tarantula's own retreat and lays an egg on it. Definitely a case of adding insult to injury! The wasp egg hatches into a little wasp grub that feeds on the flesh of the living tarantula (adult pompilid wasps eat nectar and fruit). The size of the adult wasp is correlated with the size of its larval host as the wasp can only grow when it is a larva. Because the goliath birdeating tarantula is the largest of tarantulas, its wasp nemesis is about the size of a sparrow! I have twice seen the wasps that specialize in goliath birdeater tarantulas in the French Guiana rain forest in northeastern South America.

Lifestyles of the Big and Hairy

Tarantulas need to stay at home in the safety of their silk-lined retreat during the day in order to escape the heat of the sun and predators. Tarantulas have adapted by building sophisticated silk-lined retreats. Different species have different habitat requirements for their retreats, which range from the rain forest canopy to burrows in the desert soil. You will need to keep the ecology of your tarantula in mind when you decide how to keep it. Here I have categorized these retreat types into three main types:

Opportunistic burrowers: Species that modify preexisting burrows or use crevices under environmental features such as logs or rocks for retreat construction. The actual retreat is not usually heavily lined with silk and is variable in size. Examples of opportunistic burrowers are the large South American tarantulas: goliath birdeater tarantulas, Colombian lesserblack tarantulas, and some smaller species like Haitian brown tarantulas.

Obligate burrowers: The term obligate means to be required or obliged to do something. Obligate burrowers are those species that have a specific burrow type that they construct themselves, rarely modifying preexisting structures as do the opportunistic burrowers. Examples of obligate burrowers are Mexican blond tarantulas found in the Sonoran desert as well as tropical species like Thailand black tarantulas and skeleton tarantulas. Silk use is variable. Some tarantulas extend the silk lining into a trumpet-shaped collar at the entrance that may also incorporate leaves and twigs.

Arboreals: The term arboreal means living in trees; however, as I am using it here it refers to living off the ground. Arboreal tarantulas build a silk retreat on cliff faces, road banks, and trees, as well as buildings. Arboreal tarantulas generally have specific adaptations for climbing such as broad, flattened foot surfaces on the tarsi and metatarsi. Examples are Trinidad chevron tarantulas, pinktoe tarantulas, and Trinidad mahogany tarantulas. There is a slight division of substrate use among the arboreals. For instance, pinktoe tarantulas are not known to use road banks, whereas the Trinidad chevron tarantulas do not favor foliage. Adaptable species like pinktoes may be commonly found living on agricultural crops (such as bananas and pineapples) as well as on houses and other human structures.

Tarantula Defense

No tarantula venom is known to be lethal to humans; however, while no tarantula has so far been found to be deadly, they certainly have a lot of venom and you should be very careful if you decide to handle the more aggressive species. You would not want to find out the hard way that you are sensitive to tarantula venom. There is evidence that some of the Old World species, such as the ornamental tarantulas (see Species Accounts, beginning on page 45), have more potent venom than previously known for tarantulas. At the very least, a tarantula bite should be cleaned the same way as any animal bite and kept under close watch for signs of inflammation and infection. If any systemic symptoms appear, seek immediate medical attention.

Although tarantulas possess a large amount of venom, biting is not the first line of defense for many; they rely on hiding in the security of their retreat. Most New World species also have an amazing defense against predators—they throw darts. These "darts" are called urticating hairs (urticating is a medical term that means irritating or inflaming). Tarantula urticating hairs rely on mechanical irritation, functioning like microscopic porcupine quills. Interestingly, the hairs are found only on New World tarantulas, and most New World tarantulas have them. They apparently may be very specific and some irritate the nasal passages of only small mammals, while others affect only large vertebrates like humans. There have been reports of serious eye inflammation from urticating hairs, so take great care when working with those species with more potent hairs such as the goliath birdeater or Mexican redknee tarantulas. Those species that lack the hairs, such as all those from the Old World and a few New World exceptions such as Trinidad chevron tarantulas, are far more aggressive and prone to biting. When annoyed, many tarantulas can also make a warning noise by rubbing specialized structures on the appendages together. Most of these sound-producing structures are found on the chelicerae and leg bases. An interesting exception is the goliath birdeating tarantula, which uses special hairs on the portions of its legs and pedipalps (the femora). The goliath birdeating tarantula rubs its legs and pedipalps together when annoyed, making a loud hissing noise.

A pinktoe tarantula (Avicularia avicularia) *returns to its retreat on a tree trunk. This is an example of an arboreal retreat. Most arboreal tarantulas spin tough silken tubes to hide in during the day.*

TARANTULA BASICS

Choosing a tarantula can be a lot like choosing a dog. Do you want a happy pet that is easy to get along with, such as a Golden Retriever, or are you interested in something exotic but harder to handle, such as a wolf-dog hybrid? Read on for details.

Why Do You Want a Tarantula?

Ideally, you bought this book before you bought your first tarantula and can choose your first spider based on what you want the spider for, rather than accommodating an unsuitable pet. Tarantulas, like any other group of animals, vary from species to species and individual to individual in their behavior. There are over 850 tarantula species in the world, and a large proportion of these are available from the pet trade and breeders. Unfortunately, most tarantula species are just too active and aggressive ever to handle safely; however, the good news is that many of the hardiest species also make the best pets. When I say pets, I mean animals you can handle and can keep healthy and happy in a simple, easy-to-clean cage. In contrast, keeping one of the more aggressive tarantulas is similar to keeping tropical fish in that they are beautiful animals you can admire only through glass.

So, what do you want this big, hairy spider for? When I began with tarantulas I was happy to get to see such a big, unusual critter up

A Panama blond tarantula (Psalmopoeus pulcher) rests on the side of a tree.

close, to watch it eat, and occasionally handle it. At that stage an American desert tarantula met my needs. I suggest that unless you have lots of experience with other small tropical animals with similar needs (such as small reptiles or amphibians), you begin with one of the common, hardy spiders from the southwestern United States, Central America, or Chile. This list of tarantulas includes any from the United States, the large and beautiful tarantulas in the genus *Brachypelma* from Central America like redrump tarantulas or redknee tarantulas, the pretty and hardy Costa Rican zebra tarantulas from Central America, and finally the Chilean common tarantula from Chile (see chapter on Commonly Available Species, beginning on page 41). If you and your first spider get along, then you can later diversify your collection and even try to breed your own tarantulas.

Buying a Tarantula

This is a great time to be getting interested in tarantula keeping as the variety of species available is greater than it has ever been—and getting wider. Today you can easily find species that were either totally unheard of or legendary among tarantula enthusiasts just a few years ago. Many people are breeding a wide variety of spiders, and you have the option of buying a captive-bred hatchling or a wild-caught adult. Raising a pet tarantula from hatching can be an exciting challenge, but remember to be sure of having a regular supply of small food items until it is large enough to eat the more commonly available prey species (see the section on foods and feeding, beginning on page 34). Very young tarantulas should be fed at least twice a week for optimal growth.

Beginning the Search

To begin your search for a tarantula you should try canvassing your local pet shops for the kind of tarantulas they have on hand. Most shops now carry at least some of the less-expensive types. Any store catering to the trade in reptiles should also have tarantulas. Face it, those of us who like tarantulas also tend to be intrigued with reptiles and amphibians (and vice versa). I hope you already frequent a favorite pet shop with proprietors you trust. They may be the same folks who sold you your first gerbil when you were younger. I suggest you look over the tarantulas at several stores and get a feel for the variety of spiders available. Check over the condition and temperament of the tarantulas they have. Obviously, pet shop proprietors cannot be experts on all the kinds of critters they sell; therefore, unless you are lucky, you will probably have to be self-informed.

Mail-order Tarantulas

It is always best to make a tarantula purchase in person. However, if you live in an area where no pet shops are willing to sell tarantulas or you desire one of the more unusual, hard-to-find species, you will need to turn to mail-order

dealers. If you get onto the World Wide Web and do a search using the keyword *tarantula,* you will quickly find hundreds of web sites devoted to tarantulas, including dealers. You can also look for print ads in the arachnid and reptile hobbyist magazines. Several long-term tarantula dealers with excellent reputations in the United States offer amazing selections as well as excellent expertise. Additionally, more individuals whose reliability is not yet established are also doing it on the side. Getting amazing deals buying directly from other private breeders is possible. Getting badly burned is also possible! An added advantage to forming a good relationship with a tarantula dealer is that you will have a wholesale outlet for your own spiderlings. Housing and feeding several hundred spiderlings can be a daunting task. Selling them all one or two at a time to private buyers can also be hard work. I have found it best to let the professionals sell the spiders in small numbers, and I will sell off (or offer for trade) entire clutches of tarantulas to the dealers. Dealers generally offer less than half the retail value for spiderlings in trade and slightly less (if anything) in cash. However, it can take the sting out of finding out your spiderlings are worth only 50 cents each if you can send them off in lots of 100!

Distinguishing Male from Female

When you finally go tarantula shopping, be sure you can tell an adult male from immatures and adult females. You will want to avoid buying an adult male tarantula, as males do not live nearly as long as females. This is tied to the ecology of the sexes: males leave their burrows or retreats to look for females when they mature. These males wander for miles, burn out, and then die (preferably *after* having mated). The females stay at home and conserve their energies for producing eggs. The rule so far seems to be that female tarantulas live three times as long as the males, from egg to grave. Unfortunately, it is tricky to tell the sex of immature tarantulas, as both immature males and females look and act pretty much alike.

Inspecting Your Choice

After having found several tarantulas to look over, check for missing legs, shrunken or bald abdomens, and continually pacing spiders. While tarantulas can regenerate missing legs when they molt, missing legs can be symptoms of mishandling or excessive climbing and falling in the cage. Tarantulas in nature are not athletic; they mostly just sit and wait for a hapless bug to wander by. They are the ultimate couch potatoes, and a happy tarantula is sitting still or grooming itself. A pacing spider may be exhibiting signs of maladaptation to captivity. Also, does this spider have a nice, full abdomen or is it shriveled up? Though tarantula species vary in body shape, the abdomen should always be as big or bigger than the cephalothorax. A small abdomen is also a characteristic of adult males. If it has a skinny butt, check the palps and first pair of legs again for male equipment. A good meal may be all the spider needs, but then again it may not be adapting well to captivity. Interestingly, a skinny tarantula is probably not suffering from internal parasites. Very little is known about spider pathology; however, the most common kinds of spider parasites are parasitoid wasps and flies that ultimately kill their hosts and cannot be cured. These types of internal parasites are rare, and you have less than a one-in-

The Tools of the Trade

There are three items that you will find indispensable for tarantula keeping:
✔ The first is a pair of jumbo tweezers sold by surgical supply houses and some advanced reptile suppliers. These large forceps are usually 11 inches (28 cm) long and chrome plated. They are very handy for feeding and cage cleaning. Particularly if you acquire any of the more aggressive tarantula species, a pair of these will make feeding and cleaning the cage much less exciting (and I consider the excitement of risking a tarantula bite something to avoid!).
✔ The second useful tool is a plastic pump spray bottle. These misters (or atomizers) are indispensable for humidifying a cage. You can usually buy these at any hardware or garden supply store. I strongly recommend using distilled water in tarantula cages that you spray regularly, as mineral deposits will form over time if you use tap water. Be aware that many spiders do not like being directly sprayed with a mister.
✔ The third item is a large, long-handled spoon or other kitchen utensil that can be used to remove prey remains, mix and rearrange the substrate, coax an aggressive spider to move to the back of the cage, and add new substrate.

a-hundred chance of finding your pet dead one day and a bizarre fly maggot emerging from it. There are also nematode worms that parasitize spiders, but, again, internal parasites are not the problem for tarantulas that they are for imported vertebrates.

New tarantula species appear in the pet trade regularly. This Asian beauty is called **Cyriopagopus thorelli.** *It is so far only rarely available to hobbyists.*

Bald abdomens in tarantulas can mean that the spider has a bad attitude (or is an older male). Most species of tarantulas from the New World have urticating hairs on their abdomens that they shed in defense when they are annoyed (see page 15). These hairs are replaced only when the spider molts and gets a new cuticle. All the species I recommend for beginners have urticating hairs. This is because those tarantula species that have these hairs also tend to have calmer temperaments, perhaps because they rely more on their hairs for defense than biting. Particularly reactive or high-strung tarantulas will shed these hairs at the least provocation; they will reach up with their last pair of legs and flick the hairs off with a quick brushing motion. Jittery individuals like this make poor pets if you want an animal you can handle. They are more prone to do even more unfriendly things, such as making a run for it or even biting.

Shipping Syndrome

Occasionally when you buy freshly imported tarantulas, you will be confronted with specimens that seem to be in fine health but will eventually fail to live and thrive. I have had this happen several times when I acquired tarantulas directly from importers. In all these cases, the spiders looked fine and even attacked prey. However over a period of weeks, they failed to gain weight and became weak, eventually dying. In the final stages, many of them got infestations of scuttle fly maggots around the mouth. Because no veterinarian is trained to treat spiders, the best I could do was question the importers. Based on what they told me, I could only conclude that the spiders had been badly dehydrated at some point in transit. This dehydration may have damaged their mouth and/or stomach, leading to the maggot infestations (called *myiasis*) or the damaged tissue and death. However, this is purely conjecture on my part.

Housing

Housing for a tarantula can be as elaborate as you want. One nice thing about tarantulas is that they do not destroy plants so if you are into naturalistic vivaria, spiders are perfect. On the other hand, if you want to keep it simple, tarantulas do not need much either. Because in nature tarantulas live out their lives in and around a burrow or retreat, they just do not need much room. In fact, too much room could be a disadvantage—in a large, airy cage, they may feel insecure and spend a lot of time pacing in search of a retreat. Tarantulas should always be housed alone. It is important to remember that *all* tarantulas are potential cannibals. Never put more than one individual in a cage, no matter how well fed they are; it is all but certain that one day there will only be *one* very fat spider. There are interesting exceptions to this rule for two genera of arboreal tarantula, but more about that in the following chapter.

Some people use tank dividers (marketed for fish keeping) to save on caging costs and space. This is inhumane and generally ends up being false economy. Tank dividers are a very poor idea for tarantula keeping because of the antisocial tendencies of tarantulas. These dividers are not spider proof! They are not sealed around the edge, but hang in place with clips. Eventually, one will go over or around the partition with disastrous results. If you must divide a larger tank, have a piece of glass cut to fit at a glass shop and firmly fix it in place using the type of silicon caulking sold to repair aquarium tanks.

Humidity

The first thing to keep in mind with tarantula keeping is humidity. Even tarantulas from the harshest deserts spend most of their time in deep burrows that are much cooler and moister than surface conditions. Tropical tarantulas are just not able to take extreme environmental conditions, although those from desert regions are a little hardier. So, if you are going to keep a tropical tarantula in a simple cage with no retreat, then you will have to be more careful about humidity:

The Mexican fireleg tarantula (**Brachypelma boehmi**) *is one of the most beautiful of the Mexican tarantulas.*

✔ Tarantulas must *always* have water. Even though they do not always have water in the wild, your home is not the wild and your living room in the winter is probably drier than any desert. Spiders in the wild can drink from a variety of sources, but in your living room in a cage, you have to provide the water. Some species of tarantula can go over two years with no food, but *they must have water.* I always use a shallow dish, such as a glass ashtray. Some people put a sponge in the water believing that the spider needs to suck the water from the sponge. This is not true, but one advantage of a sponge in the water is that food crickets will not drown if they fall in.

✔ Humidity should be around 70 to 80 percent for tropical species, lower for tarantulas from drier areas (40 to 50 percent). For the tropical tarantulas keep the substrate moist at all times, but not so moist that there is condensation on the inside of the cage.

✔ There should always be airflow in and out of the tank. Never totally seal a cage, such as by covering it with a piece of glass. You can control the humidity in a cage by regulating airflow. For aquaria with screen lids this can be

done by partially covering the lid with plastic and misting with a handheld sprayer of the type sold for spraying plants. It is better to use distilled water rather than tap water as the minerals in tap water will eventually leave mineral deposits on the sides of the cage. If your tarantula has a retreat the cage can be kept drier, as the air in the retreat will be moister than the ambient air. This is one of the advantages of keeping tarantulas in more naturalistic accommodations.

Temperature

The second thing to keep in mind is temperature. Tarantulas do not need to be as warm as you might think, but there are limits. For tropical species the mid to upper 70s°F (20s°C) are fine. You can keep North American tarantulas and the Chilean species cooler than this, but they will not usually eat if they get down into the 60s°F (less than 20s°C). Keeping tarantulas warmer will mean that they will eat more and, if immature, grow faster. Unfortunately, items marketed to warm up reptiles will not work well for tarantulas, as tarantulas do not like their habitat to be as warm as that of lizards. Most heat products designed for reptiles provide hot spots so the reptile can warm up and move off when it gets too warm. Unfortunately, tarantulas do not bask like lizards, so you will have to forget a hot rock. Hot rocks will also dry out a tank very quickly, leading to water stress. Using incandescent lights is risky as it will also dry the spider out. If you go this route, be very careful with bulb wattage. Use a low-watt bulb and always check the temperature with a thermometer. An undertank heater is an option, but if you use one, also use deep substrate to keep the warmth diffused. A spider will get stressed

as it gets into the mid to upper 90s°F (mid to upper 30s°C). Over 100°F (upper 30's to 40s°C) and you will have a dead spider. If you have to keep one or several tarantulas warm in the winter, try using low-watt bulbs on individual cages, or get a larger tank to place the smaller individual cages in and heat that.

You can see that keeping many tarantula species successfully means walking a thin line with regard to temperature and humidity. Temperature and humidity interact to create the climate in the cage (remember the old adage, "It ain't the heat, it's the humidity"?). Some tarantulas are more tolerant of fluctuating conditions than others. I have pointed out the species that are hardiest and those that are more finicky. Be very careful with these variables when you are housing the tropical tarantulas, as there is no getting around the importance of temperature and humidity with these animals.

Substrates

Soil

Soil is a surprisingly complicated material. It ain't just dirt! Soil varies in how much moisture it will hold and how friable it is (or how hard it becomes when it dries). Because most tarantulas live out their lives in or on the soil surface, you need to pay attention to what you put into your tarantula's cage. You can either use commercially available bagged potting soil or topsoil, or you can go dig up some natural soil to use as substrate. You have little reason to sterilize the soil because the second the soil is exposed to the air, it begins to get colonized by all the things that you were trying to kill such as mold spores and mites.

Gardeners want their potting soil sterilized to kill weed seeds, and this is not a worry for tarantula keepers. However, fungi and mites can be a problem. Surprisingly, I have found that I have had fewer problems with pests by using natural soil. This may seem counterintuitive. However, by having a natural array of soil organisms in the tank, they may keep each other in check. If you have freshly sterilized soil, the first things to colonize will take over as they have it all to themselves. For instance, the worst fungal growth I have ever had has been in cages I lined with sterilized peat moss and bark chips. In these cages, I had white, wooly looking mats of fungus growing all over the substrate. Other cages that had the same, but unsterilized, substrate had no such fungal growth. Some kinds of natural soil critters like sow bugs (or pill bugs, a crustacean in the order Isopoda) help keep a tank free of rotting prey remains and fungi. The spiders apparently will not eat them because of the chemicals they secrete as a defense. You can find sow bugs under rotting bark and under logs in a wooded area if you want to add any to your tarantula terraria.

The substrate should function as a biologically neutral bedding that retains moisture. Because tarantulas are so thrifty in their feeding habits, there is generally little waste left after they eat and excrete; therefore, you do not have to consider absorbency for wastes, only for holding water. There are several choices for bedding:

1. vermiculite
2. peat moss
3. sphagnum moss
4. bark mulch
5. potting soil.

Things never to use are any of the commercially available small-animal beddings (corn cob, pine or cedar shavings, Aspen bedding, or sawdust) or paper as these will all quickly grow mold when kept moist. Also, cedar bedding contains toxic oils that repel and kill invertebrates. Cedar is used in cedar closets for a reason—it repels moths that damage clothes.

All the substrates I recommended were developed primarily for gardening. All are potting media or are used to condition potting media, and primarily act to retain water. Thus, your best source is a well-equipped garden supply store. Many pet retailers sell moss and bark chips marketed for reptile keeping, but gardening suppliers are generally cheaper. You can often find many other things useful for tarantula rearing at a garden supply place, even if you are not interested in plants for terraria, because indoor gardeners also use cork bark, bark chips, and sheets of sphagnum moss.

Making Substrate

For cages that will not have any plants I recommend substrates mixed depending on the habits of the spider. For cages to house arboreals use 1 inch (2.5 cm) or so of bark chips to hold water for humidity. For tropical burrowers I use a soil-based mix heavy in peat moss and fine bark chips. Depending on the heaviness of the potting soil, use 60 to 80 percent peat moss. (By heaviness I mean how dark and dense the potting soil is.) If you squeeze a handful of it and release it, does it hold the shape of your hand? If it does, then it is too heavy. It should crumble when released. Adding more conditioner will solve the problem. If the tarantula is the type that readily burrows on its own, add bark chips to give the substrate structure. This structure will reduce burrow collapse. For desert spiders use peat or fine bark chips mixed about 50/50 with clean sand. The vegetable material will give the sub-strata texture and retain moisture longer (which even desert spiders need).

Recommended Products

The products sold to condition potting soil that are also useful in tarantula keeping are vermiculite, peat moss, sphagnum moss, and bark mulch (pine or cypress).

✔ *Vermiculite* is a mineral product. It is made from baked mica (a mineral) that expands to a fluffy consistency when heated. It is biologically inert, has high moisture-retaining capability, and because it is not an organic product, does not harbor any unwanted critters, such as mites.

✔ *Peat moss* is dug from peat bogs and is made up of partially decomposed bog plants.

Because bogs are very acid habitats, the plant material decomposes very slowly.

✔ *Sphagnum moss* is found growing in peat bogs but is the actual live plant harvested and dried, rather than its partially decomposed remains. Sphagnum moss is sold chopped, baled, and in sheets. Sheets of sphagnum moss are also sold in hobby stores (such as those that sell silk plants and basketmaking supplies). I find it useful for covering the soil in planted terraria.

✔ *Bark mulch* is available in a variety of grades. They are a by-product of the lumber industry and so are usually inexpensive. Most that is sold is pine bark but there is also cypress bark. All these bark products are used

The pink zebra tarantula (Eupalaestrus tenuitarsus) *is among the most docile of tarantulas. It has only recently been imported from Paraguay.*

primarily for ground cover in landscaping and all are also useful for keeping tarantulas.

✔ *Potting soil* describes a variety of mixes sold at any gardening supply or department store. They vary widely in content and suitability for tarantula keeping. Ideally, you can find a potting soil that is all or mostly pure soil, with little conditioner added. The problem is that many of the conditioners used in commercial potting soils are artificial and unattractive in terraria. Commonly used amendments are perlite (a mineral product like vermiculite made from volcanic rock), chopped cardboard waste, and even Styrofoam! However, Styrofoam and perlite are white and are an obviously unnatural substance that will detract from the appearance of the cage.

Cage Types

Tarantula housing can be any of three types:

1. pet
2. utilitarian
3. vivaria.

There are of course many permutations on this.

Pet Housing

Let's return to the hypothetical first pet tarantula from the section on buying a tarantula (see page 17). This spider is probably something like a Chilean common tarantula. You will always want to be able to see this spider and perhaps even handle it. I would recommend starting with a simple plastic cage of the type commonly sold as a pet carrier. You can also use a 1- to 5-gallon (3.8–19 L) tank. There is no point using a larger size. Buy sand or gravel to cover the bottom, some kind of water dish, and you are set. You do not want

to use any kind of small mammal bedding; these are all made to be absorbent and disposable. Tarantulas just do not eliminate very often. When they do, they pass mostly crystals of protein waste products that look like flecks of white paint. You will not have to clean this type of cage very often, maybe twice a year. The kinds of tarantulas you would keep in this cage can take the drier conditions.

Utilitarian Housing

Utilitarian housing is like the pet caging in its simplicity but with improvements for more delicate species. You will want to use this kind of caging if you start to collect more than a couple of spiders or start buying spiderlings. I use plastic boxes in two sizes, small and large. The best kinds are the type made of polystyrene and marketed as shoe and sweater storage boxes. The advantage of polystyrene is that it is almost as clear as glass, so you can peer in. The flip side is that it is also almost as breakable as glass. For this reason you may have trouble finding any for sale, as too many arrive at the store broken and retailers are switching to the softer kinds of plastic box (which are also almost totally opaque). You can use whatever type of substrate that is suitable for the spider: sandy mixes for desert animals, something peaty for jungle spiders. You can control humidity in these boxes by making a number of ventilation holes. I do this by melting the holes with a soldering iron. If you use this method, be sure to do it outside or in some well-ventilated area, as the fumes are obnoxious if not actually harmful. I also put in a piece of cork bark for a retreat. It is especially important to keep up with cage maintenance with these kinds of cages. Take out prey

Inside the Tarantula Mind

The very thought that a tarantula might have feelings at all may seem like an idea from the lunatic fringe. However tarantulas, like any animal, have motivations (referred to as drives in the jargon of animal behavior) and desires (or appetites). So, when I say feelings here, I do not mean that tarantulas can suffer or feel happiness the way people or some of the larger animals can. Rather, tarantulas do have behaviors directed at fulfilling their biological needs such as seeking water when thirsty or finding prey when hungry. While the desires of a tarantula are surely very primitive, if you frustrate these desires, the spider does not flourish and may even die. You may find it easy to accept the idea that if a tarantula needs water, and you fail to provide it, the spider will eventually die. However, what if the spider needs a secure hiding place? The first need is physiological, the second need, behavioral.

I have come to believe that one of the great limits on the successful keeping and rearing of tarantulas comes from failing to consider the behavioral needs of the spider. To understand the tarantula's behavioral needs, you need to consider its habits in the wild. All tarantulas live their lives centered on a secure hiding place they find, modify, and line with silk and to which they always return after hunting.

From what I have observed in the wild and in captivity, I have come to believe that tarantulas divide the world into two places: inside the retreat, and outside the retreat. I say this because:

1. they invest a lot of energy and silk in retreat construction and maintenance;

2. they behave differently when outside the retreat than when inside;

3. if you deprive a tarantula in captivity of the opportunity to have a retreat, it may pace and climb about the cage, sometimes to the point of injury; and finally

4. tarantulas in the wild and in captivity keep their retreats clean. They take great care to dispose of prey remains and shed skins outside the retreat and defecate elsewhere.

So, if you keep a tarantula in a small container, like a plastic box, it may come to act as if the container is a large retreat with no exit. Your tarantula will line the box with silk, it will attempt to remove prey remains by pushing them into the corner, and it may dash around wildly when you open the lid (imagine how you would feel if some giant suddenly ripped open the ceiling in your bedroom and peered in!). On the other hand, if you keep the same tarantula in a large cage, such as a 10-gallon (40 L) tank with a screen lid, with no place to build a retreat, the tarantula will pace, sit huddled in the corner, and run for it when you open the top.

Of course, a lot of what happens will depend on the species' or even the individual spider's temperament. You can generally keep a Chilean common tarantula in the most barren cage and it will seem to do just fine, or you may keep a pinktoe tarantula this way because it will build its own retreat entirely out of silk. However, condemning any of the more high-strung, moisture-sensitive species such as a goliath birdeater tarantula or Cameroon red tarantula to a barren, well-lit, dry cage is inhumane at best and a death sentence at worst. It can even be unsafe to keep some of the more active arboreal spiders without a retreat. If you keep a Togo starburst tarantula or an ornamental tarantula in a barren container, it will generally become agitated when you open the cage to feed or water it. You may soon have it running up your arm and across your face. (I *hate* when that happens!) If, on the other hand, you provide your tarantula with a secure retreat, the startled spider will either run into the retreat or sit tight in the retreat when you open the cage.

The quality of life for the spider becomes even more crucial when you set out to breed tarantulas. You just cannot breed all tarantula species in a plastic shoe box with a bit of substrate on the bottom. Many spiders just need a little privacy, and this means providing them with the opportunity to build a retreat. Unfortunately, tarantulas appear to have only a very limited ability to adapt to captive conditions. These are wild animals, and you need to adapt the conditions to them. So, call me crazy, but you will find that if you consider your tarantula's feelings when you design its accommodations, you will have much greater success in keeping *and* breeding a wide range of species.

Utilitarian housing for a tarantula. This plastic box of the kind marketed to store shoes is modified to house a tarantula. Note the air holes melted in the plastic. The number of air holes you make can be varied depending on the moisture requirements of the tarantula.

remains as soon as can or you will have fungi and pests in the cage.

Vivaria

Here you can have some fun, but you will have to be content with seeing your spider only once in a while. The idea of a vivarium is to try to make a tiny piece of natural habitat; however, as in the wild, you will have to hunt for your spider at night if you want to see it because it will be in its retreat out of sight

most of the time. I feel that the thrill of seeing the spider sitting in the evening at the entrance to its burrow or retreat as it would in the wild is worth the wait, but you be the judge. Some types of more high-strung species may not thrive or even survive if you try to deprive them of the security of a natural retreat. Remember that, in the wild, tarantulas spend

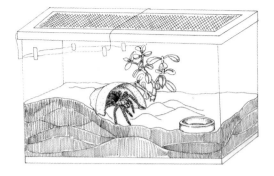

A simple vivarium set-up for an opportunistic burrower. Almost anything can be used for an artificial retreat. Here a clay flower pot broken in half length-wise is home. For most tropical spiders, the air flow in a cage with a screen top would lead to a stressfully dry environment. You can counteract this with regular misting with distilled water and by partially covering the screen lid plastic, as you see here.

most of their time in a snug, silk-lined burrow or arboreal retreat. Some individual tarantulas just cannot get used to life in a plastic box. To breed tarantulas you may need to attempt a naturalistically set-up cage to succeed. These kinds of cages can be built based on the ecology of the spiders they are to house.

Housing for Opportunistic Burrowers

Opportunistic burrowers are fairly easy to please. These tarantulas adopt a preexisting shelter in the wild and modify it for their use. At its simplest, a cage will have a layer of soil and mulch 3 to 8 inches (7.6–20 cm) deep with a shelter built like a cave. I use pieces of cork bark, which are ideal. You could also use tree bark, a flat rock, or a flowerpot broken in half lengthwise. Bury the shelter in the tank so that there is a low level of dirt (where the water dish goes) in front of the entrance and a pile of dirt on top of the retreat to make an upper level. I usually partially fill the cave with dirt so that the spider has to dig the substrate out and shape the burrow to meet its individual needs. You can tell you have been successful the morning after you put in the tarantula when you look in the cage and see dirt pushed

out of the new retreat by the spider. Some spiders will take over the artificial retreat the first night; some will take days or weeks to do it. Some never do. You can plant small, low light-tolerant houseplants and cover the soil surface with decorator's sphagnum moss that comes in sheets and can be spread out like a carpet, and/or cover the soil with fine bark chips. Plants are certainly an option but will enhance the appearance of the cage and help moderate the humidity. I do not believe the spiders care.

Housing for Obligate Burrowers

Housing obligate burrowers naturalistically is a little trickier than for opportunistic burrowers. The biggest problem is that these spiders dig their own burrows and conditions have to be right to induce burrowing. Also, the condition of the soil has to be ideal, or the burrow will not maintain its shape and collapse. In other words, just pouring dirt into a tank and putting in the spider won't work. Your best bet is to build a burrow and hope the spider will move in. I have had better success doing this with tropical rain forest spiders than with North American desert burrowers. You can use florists' foam (a synthetic material) that comes in

Obligate burrowers can be more tricky to house as many species, particularly those from desert regions, have finicky burrow-site requirements. One possibility is to offer them an artificial burrow.

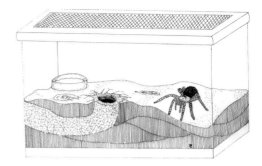

blocks and can be cut. In either case, the idea is to construct a tunnel just big enough to admit the spider. If the spider needs more room, it will make the tunnel bigger itself. Another alternative is plastic pipe of various kinds. Some obligate burrowers (especially the African species) are such active burrowers that they will make their own burrow from scratch if you give them

Greenbottle blue tarantula **(Chromatopelma cyaneopubescens).** *The only species of tarantula where the immatures, adult females, and adult males are all colored an iridescent blue.*

a deep bed of peat moss and bark chips. If the spider does not make any attempts to burrow, you might want to try to check if the cage is well ventilated. If the vivaria is too snug, the spider may feel it is already in a large burrow, and not be motivated to get under cover. By increasing daytime light levels or making the cage better ventilated you can give it a hint. Be careful not to stress it, if it doesn't want to burrow, you can't force it!

Plants in the Vivarium

Plants can make a tarantula cage an intriguing piece of tropical habitat in your home; however, plants can also be tricky to maintain in a tarantula cage. Very few plants are suitable for planting in a tarantula habitat. One of the great limits to plant growth is light but too much light can stress a tarantula.

Types of Plants

Plants I have had success with are snake plants (in the genus *Sansevieria*), climbing plants, such as philodendrons or pothos (either small-leaved *Philodendron* sp. or *Epipremnum aureum*), small bromeliads (*Cryptanthus* sp.), and some peperomias (*Peperomia* sp.). The trick is to combine toughness, tolerance of low light levels, and small size.

Examples of common houseplants that would not work in a tank would be jade plants (which need lots of light), fig trees (which need lots of light and grow too big), and spider plants (again, these need lots of light).

Snake plants come in a variety of sizes, can be pruned, and tolerate virtual darkness. One particularly useful type is the cultivated variety 'Hahnii' (*Sansevieria trifasciata* 'Hahnii'), which stays small. There are several types of vining plant that are useful. One of these, pothos (*Epipremnum aureum*), is extremely durable and tolerant of low-light levels. In fact, you will have trouble killing this one. Some species of philodendron are also suitable. The bromeliad *Cryptanthus* spp. is sometimes hard to find but well worth the search. It is marketed as "earth star" or "starfish plant." These are small and tolerant of low-light levels. They come in varying shapes and shades of red, white, and green. Peperomias (*Peperomia* spp.) come in a variety of sizes and colors and are often small enough to suit a tarantula cage. To avoid the risk of overheating from putting a cage near a window, I would use a fluorescent light fixture to light the cage. Any of the light fixtures sold for aquaria will work.

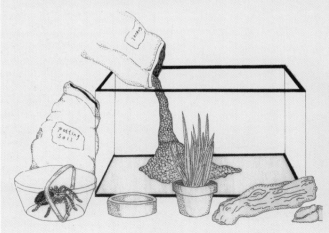

Tarantulas do very well in a planted vivarium. There are two modifications you will need to make to the simple cage setup in order to accommodate the plants. The first is a layer of gravel under the soil to allow for proper drainage. Without this the plant roots may drown, killing the plant. The second is adequate light that is not too hot or bright for the tarantula. A fluorescent light of the type marketed for aquaria is suitable.

Housing dangers: An important point to keep in mind with these larger cages is that tarantulas can accidentally hang themselves in tall tanks. Tarantulas have two claws on each foot and these can become caught on the screen top or edges of the tank top. The hapless spider cannot release itself and it will hang there until you free it. It can hurt itself in the fall. If you have a spider that paces a lot, climbing up the corners of the tank, you are likely to find it swinging one morning. One way to minimize the problem is to use shallow tanks and fill them with enough substrate so that the spider can reach the floor of the cage with its back legs and the top with its front.

Housing for Arboreals

The arboreal tarantulas are the easiest of all to set up naturalistically as they build their own retreat. The trickiest part relates to the fact that the spiders are arboreal and want to go up when they look for a site to build a home. "Up" usually means at the corner made by the wall and lid of the tank. If they do this, you will destroy their retreat every time you open the cage. There are a couple of ways around this: Make the top the side, or try to entice them to build elsewhere in the cage. It is handy to stand a 10-gallon (37.9 L) terraria with a screen lid on one end and let the spider build at the top. If you do this you will have to make some kind of dam in the front of the cage so the substrate does not spill onto the floor when you open the cage. This can be a cut piece of plastic or wood held in place by pressure or silicon caulking. The alternative is to build a tempting nook for a retreat using pieces of bark leaning against the wall of the tank. I have had success making a lean-to with

a couple of pieces of cork bark. When the spider initially inspects the tank, it will be drawn to the snug spot between the bark slabs. Possibly, here is where the spider will build its retreat. As a last resort you can use the harassment technique. If you keep destroying an inconveniently located retreat, the spider will try a new spot. Eventually, even a tarantula can take a hint.

Cage Pests

There are often critters that make a pest of themselves in tarantula cages. This is almost entirely a problem in the moister cages, as dry cages are just too inhospitable. The worst pests are mites and scuttle flies. Neither is likely to be a direct threat to the tarantula but are a nuisance.

Mites

Mites are exceptions to the rule that arachnids are not economically important. They are also the only arachnid group that is not almost entirely predatory. In fact, mites are so important ecologically that they have their own branch of science called acarology—the study of mites and ticks. There are mites that live as parasites on other arthropods, including spiders. Fortunately, these are fairly rare in tarantula collections. However, there are common mites that are scavengers that can create problems in tarantula cages. Scavenging mites can have amazing population explosions in tarantula cages that are kept too moist and have a food source. These mites are feeding on uneaten dead prey and prey remains. Mites can come from anything put into the cage such as prey, dirt, mulch, branches, and plants—the list goes

on and on. If conditions are just right, you have a mite infestation. Mites at low population levels may never be seen or be a cause for concern; if they get on a tarantula, the tarantula can groom them off. However, occasionally the mites get the upper hand. They can attack a molting tarantula or one otherwise unable to get them off. Some types of mites spend a period of time attached to a larger creature while very young to disperse. In captivity, these hitchhikers can enter the book lungs of the tarantula and cause problems for the spider resulting from irritation and restricted air flow. There is no way to guarantee that there are no mites in any cage; they are just too ubiquitous. However, you can keep the mites under control:

✔ Keep picking up after the spider; do not let prey remains or dead crickets accumulate in the cage.

✔ Dry terraria housing desert tarantulas are not as prone to infestation. Because they are

The stunning New Guinea tarantula (Chilocosmia dichromata) *is rarely seen on dealer's price lists.*

so small, mites are even more sensitive to dry conditions than tarantulas. Occasionally let normally moist terraria dry out (keeping a full water dish at all times!).

✔ I have noticed that when mite populations are building up, they aggregate on dead crickets and the mite-infested prey can be removed, mites and all. If you get a mite infestation in a simple cage, the best bet is to strip the cage and clean it immediately. Put the infested cage in the freezer, clean it well, and put in fresh substrate. A dilute bleach-water solution can be used to sterilize the cage. Rinse it and air it out well as the chlorine gas fumes are harmful. Unfortunately, the no-pest strips that reptile keepers use will not do because they would kill the tarantula too!

✔ If your infestation is in a planted terrarium, remove the spider and let the tank dry out. This will reduce the mite infestation but will never eliminate it. It has also been shown that predatory mites used for mite control on crops can be used, but these would probably never entirely eradicate the pest mite.

Mites that are actually parasites on the spider are rare and I have only seen this once on tarantulas. I once had mites infesting arboreal tarantula spiderlings (pinktoe and Trinidad chevron tarantulas), which were killing the spiders. This mite was much smaller than the kind of mites that infest tanks as scavengers. The mites would congregate at the joints of the spider's legs where the cuticle is thin and soft and also in the book lungs. The best I could do was remove the spider from its container immediately after a shed, when many of the mites were still on the old skin, and put it in another jar (I was using baby food jars with sphagnum moss for housing). Another technique was to dust the spiderling with baby powder, applying it with a paintbrush. The talcum powder would dry out the mites, but the spider could drink. I eventually got the mites under control and was able to rear out some of the spiderlings.

Scuttle Flies

Another common pest of tarantula cages is the scuttle fly (family Phoridae, *Megacelia scalaris*). These flies are about the size of a fruit fly but are gray and prefer running to flying, hence their name. Scuttle flies are scavengers and their maggots feed on anything dead. These annoying flies are everywhere and can invade your tarantula cages from an open window in the summer. They are also associated with domestic cricket rearing.

Phorids Attacking Spiders

Occasionally, scuttle flies will lay eggs on outwardly healthy-looking tarantulas. I have occasionally found long-term captive tarantulas covered in scuttle fly eggs with a group of flies loitering in the box. The end result of this infestation is death as the maggots enter the mouth of the spider and kill it by eating it from the inside out. Unfortunately, I have no idea what leads to the female flies laying eggs onto the spiders. Normally, the flies are attracted to the smell of rotting prey. The best you can do with the scuttle flies is to control their numbers by preventing them from breeding. I have also had limited success by trapping them. I do this by putting some rotting crickets or raw meat into a jar with a small hole in the lid. The flies enter to feed and lay eggs but cannot easily get out. I periodically place this jar into a freezer to kill the flies (usually once a day) and then put it out again to catch more flies. You can imagine that the contents of this jar get pretty nasty, but it works.

Scuttle fly maggots are able to feed and grow on even the smallest amount of prey remains. If you leave any uneaten food in a moist tarantula cage, you will soon find it seething with maggots. The best tools in scuttle fly control are dryness and cleanliness. If the food dries out, the maggots die. Again, as for the mites, cleanliness is the best control method.

Fungus Gnats

One little fly you may get in your tanks are fungus gnats (flies in the family Cecidiomyiidae). These are harmless little flies that are very small and dark. They are much darker and smaller than either scuttle flies or fruit flies and seem to be all wings and legs. The larvae feed

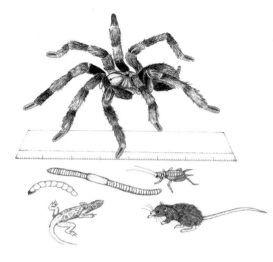

A good rule of thumb to follow in offering food to a tarantula is that the body length of the prey be less than half the body length of the tarantula.

ted to the legs of the spider. The vibrations travel up the legs, causing the cuticle to flex. This flexion of the cuticle is what is sensed by the slit sensillae. It is hard to imagine that such faint signals could be picked up and acted on by the spider! The vibratory sense is so acute that spiders can immediately tell the size and location of the prey and attack. They can also decide if the prey is too large and ignore it. I have seen tarantulas respond to my footsteps from across the room and reenter their retreat (I did not take this too personally). This information on spider senses will tell you two things: 1) prey offered must be alive, and 2) it must not be too big. Occasionally a tarantula will feed on a dead food item (see page 35). They are apparently able to recognize the food by its taste when they contact it with their feet. This is worth a try, as being able to feed a tarantula dead prey would make life much easier, since food could be stored in the freezer for later use. This would also make it safer for the spider to offer it prey that, if alive, might bite the spider, such as rodents.

on rotting plant material and cause no trouble in terraria. So if you see small, black, wispy-looking flies in your terraria, do not panic. They may just be these harmless scavengers.

Tarantula Food

Tarantulas, like most spiders, are not picky eaters. They are stimulated to feed by the motion of the prey. Even though they have eight eyes, tarantulas are basically blind and can tell only light and dark and see big shapes looming.

Perceiving Prey

Tarantulas first perceive prey using the vibrations in the surface they are standing on made by the prey as it moves around. Tarantulas do this by using sense organs on their legs called slit sensillae. The process is amazing to contemplate. The vibrations in the floor of the cage made by a walking cricket are transmit-

Diet

The key to a healthy tarantula is a diverse diet. Laboratory studies conducted by myself and others with wolf spiders have shown that no one prey species alone can be a complete diet. However, attention to diet is much more important for rearing baby tarantulas than simply maintaining an adult spider. There is no evidence yet that vitamin supplements are useful for spider rearing, but no one has looked. For most tarantulas in most situations the domestic gray cricket *(Acheta domestica)* is the staple food of choice. You can usually buy crickets at the store where you bought the tarantula; you can also find them at bait shops. Just about any bait bug can also be tarantula food: wax moth larvae, mealworms, superworms, and even earthworms.

Dead Food

I have found through trial and error that most tarantulas will eat dead food items. When it does work, feeding dead prey is a great little trick for feeding the larger spiders as you can feed a single frozen and thawed mouse to several spiders by cutting it up. This is a lot cheaper and more humane than feeding your spiders live mice or lizards. Cutting up a mouse sounds unappetizing, but if you are up to it, it is easiest to do with a knife when the mouse is still partly frozen. Just drop the partly frozen mouse chunks into the spider's cage in the evening. After it thaws, the spider will pick it up and eat. Remember to get the leftovers out of the cage the next day as the smell is unforgettable!

Amounts and Schedule

The amounts and schedule of feeding will depend on the tarantula species, age and time since last molt, and the temperature. Some species have higher metabolisms and need to eat more often than others. Examples of hungry species are the Old World spiders and the larger South American tarantulas. Examples of species with more modest food needs are the desert tarantulas of the United States and Central America and Chile. Species like these may suddenly go "off feed" and apparently think nothing of fasting for several months. Feeding rates are correlated with the life cycle of the spider: fast-growing species that mature in two to three years in general eat more than the slow-growing species that take up to 10 years to mature.

The fasting record for a spider is a tarantula from Kansas that went without food for over two years. Do not try this at home! Young tarantulas will of course eat more than old tarantulas and you cannot overfeed a growing spider. In fact the more you feed a young tarantula, the faster and larger it will grow. On the other hand, adults of those species with a slower metabolism can become spectacularly overweight and may be at risk of injuring themselves as they try to hold up their huge abdomens. Spiders are all hungrier after a molt, even if they are already full grown. It may take a few weeks for some to recover from the ordeal of molting, but then they will suddenly have renewed interest in food. Spiders preparing to molt will also lose interest in eating (see the section on molting on page 36).

It is recommended that you offer food in small amounts regularly once a week for most spiders (more often for younger animals). Watch the food—if the spider does not eat it overnight, take it out and try later. If you have an adult female of one of the desert spiders that has gone off its feed, you need to offer food only every few weeks until it is interested again. Tarantulas almost never have feeding problems; however, if they stop eating and you feel it has gone on too long (say, over a month), there are several things to check:

1. Is the spider preparing to molt?

2. Has the environment cooled off, for instance, is this happening in the fall?

3. Does the spider look thin?

4. Is the spider pacing the cage at night?

If it is either of the first two, the answer is straightforward. If the spider is in its premolt lethargy, then all you can do is wait until it molts. If the temperature in the cage has dropped, try to warm the cage. If the tarantula is native to a seasonal environment, you can also withhold food until the spring.

If it is one of the second two alternatives, things could be more serious. Whether a spider is thin or not will be based on the individual spider. If you have had it a while, you can most likely judge its weight based on how big its abdomen is relative to the rest of its body. The problem could be stress of some kind or indications of a parasite that is interfering with the spider's appetite. You could try to change the caging if the animal is also pacing a lot. I have seen wonderful changes in attitude with a new cage. Sometimes a deeper retreat

will help. Finally, remember that tarantulas are capable of amazing feats of self-imposed fasting, so do not panic if the spider is plump, quiet, and otherwise appears normal.

The Molt

It is impossible to overestimate the significance of the molt to a spider. At this time the tarantula is under extreme stress due to the hormonal changes it is going through. Try to imagine what it is like to shed your entire skin at once, including the lining of your mouth, stomach, and respiratory organs, and even the lining of the sexual organs (for adult female tarantulas). It is mind-boggling! Spiders are soft and very vulnerable just after a molt and until the cuticle hardens they are absolutely helpless. This stressful event is accompanied by renewal as this is when spiders heal, even replacing lost legs. Bald abdomens are resplendent again with a new coating of hairs, replacing those lost due to defensive shedding.

The shed cycle is mediated by a hormone called ecdysone (for the technical name for the shedding process, ecdysis). The spider has no control over the molt; when it is time to shed, it sheds. In the weeks prior to the shed you may notice that the spider loses interest in food and becomes less active, as the spider is growing a new skin beneath the old one. Just before the actual molt you can see the skin darken slightly. This is the only time when a bald abdomen is advantageous, as you can clearly see the skin that is normally a grayish

A recently molted Costa Rican zebra tarantula sits beside its shed skin.

Molting is a major event in the life of a tarantula. Here you can see that the carapace has popped up, and the spider is drawing its legs out of the old skin.

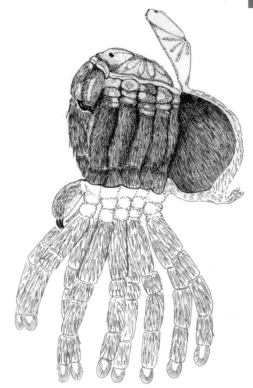

pink become darker and darker as the new cuticle forms underneath. At this time make sure there are no food items walking around in the cage, as they might take advantage of the helpless spider to turn the tables and take a bite. Also pay extra attention to humidity as tarantulas can become stuck in the old skin if they are kept too dry.

There are several behavioral cues to let you know the spider is about to shed: loss of interest in food, spinning lots of silk to make a shedding platform, and, in the hours before the actual event, rolling over on its back. Many tarantulas spin a silk mat on which they shed. Some tarantula species coat this silk sheet with urticating hairs in an effort to lose external parasites with the old skin, even if they do not have the parasites in captivity. Almost all tarantulas shed lying on their backs. Many neophyte tarantula keepers have been startled to see their new pet lying on its back with its feet in the air, apparently dead! It is crucial to leave the shedding spider absolutely alone. If disturbed, it might right itself and then shed in an unnatural position, causing problems. At the actual molt the spider will pop the carapace up like a lid and push the old skin up off the legs. At this point it will be very pale, even white in younger specimens. The cuticle will darken as it hardens. This is due to the chemical processes going on, termed "tanning." The color of arthropod cuticle is in part due to its structure, rather than pigment, which is why we never see albino insects or spiders.

The length of time it takes a spider to recover from the molt varies depending on the size of the spider. Larger spiders, in general, have thicker cuticle and lower metabolisms than smaller spiders. Very young spiderlings may be up and feeding in a day; large adults may take weeks to get over it. If you remove the shed skin soon after the molt, it will still be soft and pliable. If you then position it in a lifelike pose, when it dries it will look almost like a tarantula. This will be your best chance to examine the external anatomy of the spider, and is also one way to keep a record of the growth of your spider (see page 95 for a discussion of problems during molting).

HOW-TO: HANDLING YOUR

Caution

You should consider that tarantulas are not social animals like dogs or cats. This means that they never like being handled and there is always the chance of getting bitten by an annoyed tarantula while handling it. Although, in general, tarantula venom is not particularly toxic to humans, a bite could be very serious. There is mounting evidence that some genera of tarantulas have nastier venom than others. Do not be a guinea pig! There is always the chance of an allergic reaction such as some people have to beestings. In any case, the bite itself would be very painful. However, tarantulas, like most animals, have ways to let you know they are not in the mood to be bothered and may bite. Hair shedding, rearing up, striking out with the front pair of legs are all ways in which a tarantula says "bug off!" So, pay attention to your spider. There are several ways to handle a tarantula:

1. *free handling*, where you have the spider walk over your open hand;

2. *restrained*, where you actually pick the spider up; and

3. *hands-off*, where you induce the spider to walk into a container such as a plastic box.

Free Handling

If you have a calm tarantula (and if you are pretty calm yourself), it is easy to get it to walk onto your hand. The idea is simple—just put one hand open in front of the tarantula in its cage and give it a gentle prod in the rear end. The spider should just walk onto your open palm. Most spiders will slowly continue to walk, and so you can let it walk from hand to hand until one (or both) of you gets tired. If you are doing this for the first time, be sure you either have your hands in the cage, or sit on the floor and do this close to the ground. If the spider gets rattled and makes a run for it, you don't want it to fall to the floor.

Restrained Handling

It is very handy to be able to just reach in and pick up a tarantula; however, this is the trickiest way of all because, if you do not get a good grip the first time, you will have a really annoyed tarantula to contend with and an excellent chance of being bitten. The restrained hold consists of gently pressing down on the carapace of the spider with your index finger, and (again, *gently*) firmly grasping the sides of the cephalothorax between the second and third pair of legs with your thumb and middle finger and picking it up. Once the tarantula's feet are off the ground, it usually stops struggling and just hangs there. Do not do this with a feisty spider as, in the final analysis, they are faster than you and the one grabbed could be you. The restrained hold is only really useful to examine the underside of the tarantula.

Docile tarantulas can be coaxed onto an open palm with a gentle nudge from behind. Never free-handle a tarantula if you are not sure of its disposition. A tarantula bite could be very serious.

TARANTULA

Hands-off Handling

When all else fails, get a cup or plastic container and take control of the situation. Tarantulas are virtually blind and behave predictably. If you put a container on its side in front of the spider and prod the spider (*not* with your fingers!) in the rear, it will usually walk (or dart) in. Then you can pop the lid on and *voila!* the spider is under control. Only the truly scariest of tarantulas (such as some of the arboreal African species) are hard to handle even this way. Two things to remember, when the hair flies and you are trying to contain a fractious spider:

1. Tarantulas behave in predictable ways, and

2. they have a very limited ability to sustain physical activity.

The first point means that with experience you can predict what spiders will do in a given situation as there are few alternatives. They are just too mentally limited to sit and scheme or try and second-guess your next move. For

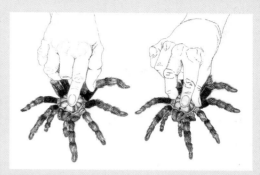

It is possible to pick up a docile tarantula using the restrained hold, but this is risky as the tarantula will respond to this as if being attacked. This hold is only useful for examining the underside of a fairly calm spider. Do not attempt this with any tarantula you would not feel comfortable free-handling or you may get bitten!

instance, one of the behavioral traits of tarantulas on the run is their habit of running up something when startled. This is true even for burrowing species. What this means is that a tarantula you are handling may run up your arm in an attempt to get away from your hands. (No, this makes no sense at all, I know.) Needless to say, it is quite nerve-wracking to have a fractious spider heading for your face; however, you can use this habit to your advantage and place the container higher than the spider, and let it climb in. The second point refers to the limited aerobic capacity of tarantulas. This brings us back to the relative inefficiency of book lungs (see page 11). The result is that even a scared tarantula will not run far because it will run out of breath. Tarantulas usually stop as soon as they get their back to the wall and huddle there, waiting for your next move.

The safest way to handle a tarantula is not to handle it at all. When in doubt use the hands-off method, using a forceps or pencil to coax the spider into a container.

COMMONLY AVAILABLE SPECIES

In choosing a tarantula as a pet, there are a number of species options to choose from. Use this chapter to see which might be best for you.

Understanding Systematics

Systematics is the scientific study of species' evolutionary relationships. Species are considered to be the only natural unit in any classification scheme because individual species can be defined using the characteristics of natural populations of organisms. Several definitions exist for the term "species." However, for sexually reproducing organisms such as tarantulas, we can define a species as a population of actually or potentially interbreeding individuals (the biological species concept of Ernst Mayr). Obviously, putting two closely related species together into a cage and inducing them to breed is cheating if they are not found together in nature. For instance, unscrupulous zoos have hybridized lions and tigers, but we can safely say that lions and tigers are separate species.

A good deal of progress has been made in refining the old hierarchical classification system that was invented before evolution was

The Mexican bloodleg tarantula (Aphonopelma bicoloratum) is one of the most stunningly colored of all tarantulas.

widely accepted as the natural process generating species diversity. Current phylogenetic analyses create many more levels, reflecting the better understanding of the branching of the spider family tree. However, with this better understanding comes increasing complexity. Currently, the spider family tree has three main branches. The Mesothelae contains the family Liphistiidae. The Opisthothele further divides into the Araneomorphae, or the true spiders, and the Mygalomorphae which contains tarantulas and their kin. The liphistiids are a very interesting group because they are the most primitive of all living spiders. Among their many primitive traits are overlapping plates on the dorsum (top) of their abdomen and that they live in burrows with trapdoors. They are found only in tropical Asia. The Araneomorphae contain all the spider species (over 34,000 species!) considered to be the typical spiders: wolf spiders, jumping spiders, orbweaving spiders, and so on. Our friends the mygalomorphs include the theraphosids, or tarantulas, and the 14 other mygalomorph families. Most of these other mygalomorphs are small, drably colored, and rarely seen in nature. Trapdoor spiders and

List of Tarantula Species Covered in the Text

Subfamily	Genus Species	Common Name
Ischnocolinae	*Heterothele villosela*	Tanzanian dwarf tarantula
Ornithoctoninae	*Cyriopagopus paganus*	Asian chevron tarantula
	Haplopelma albostriatum	Thailand zebra tarantula
	Haplopelma lividum	cobalt blue tarantula
	Haplopelma minax	Thailand black tarantula
Harpactirinae	*Ceratogyrus bechuanicus*	curvedhorn tarantula
	Ceratogyrus cornuatum	straighthorned tarantula
	Eucratoscelus longipes	African redrump tarantula
	Pterinochilus murinus	Mombassa golden starburst tarantula
Eumenophorinae	*Citharischius crawshayi*	king baboon tarantula
	Heteroscodra maculata	Togo starburst tarantula
	Hysterocrates gigas	Cameroon red tarantula
	Stromatopelma calceatum	red featherleg tarantula
Selenocosmiinae	*Coremiocnemus* sp.	Malaysian black velvet tarantula
	Chilobrachys sp.	mustard tarantula
	Poecilotheria fasciata	Sri Lankan ornamental tarantula
	Poecilotheria regalis	Indian ornamental tarantula
	Psalmopoeus cambridgei	Trinidad chevron tarantula
	Psalmopoeus irminia	Suntiger tarantula
	Selenocosmia javanensis	Java yellowknee tarantula
Theraphosinae	*Acanthoscurria geniculata*	Brazilian whiteknee tarantula
	Aphonopelma chalcodes	Mexican blond tarantula
	Aphonopelma seemanni	Costa Rican zebra tarantula
	Aphonopelma spp.	tarantulas found in the United States
	Brachypelma albopilosum	curlyhair tarantula
	Brachypelma emilia	Mexican redleg tarantula
	Brachypelma smithi	Mexican redknee tarantula
	Brachypelma vagans	Mexican redrump tarantula
	Hapalopus incei	Trinidad olive tarantula
	Chromatopelma cyaneopubescens	greenbottle blue tarantula
	Grammostola rosea	Chilean common tarantula
	Lasiodora parahybana	Brazilian salmon tarantula
	Lasiodorides polycuspulatus	Peruvian blond tarantula
	Lasiodorides striatus	Andean stripeleg tarantula
	Megaphobema robustum	Colombian giant tarantula
	Megaphobema velvetosoma	Ecuadorian brownvelvet tarantula

	Pamphobeteus antinuos	Bolivian blueleg tarantula
	Paraphysa manicata	dwarf rose tarantula
	Phormictopus cancerides	Haitian brown tarantula
	Theraphosa blondi	goliath birdeater tarantula
	Xenesthis immanis	Colombian lesserblack tarantula
Aviculariinae	Avicularia avicularia	pinktoe tarantula
	Avicularia versicolor	Antilles pinktoe tarantula
	Ephebopus murinus	skeleton tarantula
	Tapinauchenius gigas	orange treespider tarantula
	Tapinauchenius plumipes	Trinidad mahogany tarantula

funnelweb spiders are examples. In general, tarantulas are the largest, most diverse, and the most brightly marked of the mygalomorph spiders. The notion that tarantulas are primitive may, in fact, apply to most of the mygalomorph families. However, this contention does not hold up when you begin to consider the 850+ species of tarantula!

While we have a current biological basis with which to define species, reconstructing the evolutionary relationships of tarantula species and grouping them into meaningful genera or subfamilies is a lot harder. This is because these species groupings should reflect the degree of evolutionary relatedness and we get to see only the end product of millions of years of evolution, not the evolutionary process itself. While some groupings are clear (such as *Avicularia* and *Tapinauchenius* being more closely related to each other than either is to *Ceratogyrus*), the exact branching patterns of the tarantula family tree are still poorly known. Because these groupings are created by systematists who each use slightly different types of evidence and methods of analysis, the details of the interrelationships will vary from researcher to researcher, particularly the closer

you get to the species level. This is why you will see alternative schemes in different publications. Relax, take a deep breath, and rest assured that sometime before the end of the millennium it will all be sorted out.

The traits used to group tarantula species have traditionally been based on the comparison of physical features (called morphological traits). More recently, systematists working on other animal groups have also compared behavior patterns and molecular evidence (based on the comparison of proteins or DNA). Perhaps one day these tools will be applied to the problem of tarantula systematics as well. Originally, classification was a system of naming organisms and was based on the overall similarity of physical appearance. Only in the last century have systematists worked to understand species relationships by studying the evolution of specific traits. Current classification schemes should reflect the evolutionary relationships between species, genera, and higher groups. Systematics is not just a matter of naming names but a means to understand evolution itself—how the fantastic diversity of life on earth came to be.

The use of scientific names has rules. These names are always based on the rules of Latin or

The small Tanzanian chestnut tarantula (Heterothele villosela) *is interesting both because of its phylogenetic position and because of its web building ability.*

Classical Greek. The taxon names for the genus (plural, *genera*) and higher always start with a capital letter if used in full, for example, the family Theraphosidae. However, if you use the name descriptively, you use a lowercase and omit the ending, for example, theraphosid spider. This is also true for Mygalomorphae versus mygalomorph spider or Theraphosinae versus theraphosine tarantula. The genus and species names are always italicized, and the latter is lowercased. For instance, the genus and species of the cobalt blue tarantula is the *Haplopelma lividum.*

The naming of new species has a long and venerable tradition going back hundreds of years. Taxonomists, or those who identify and name species, have their own terminology and set of rules. As it stands now, you can describe a new species of anything as long as your description is published in a forum that is widely accessible in libraries. Species descriptions do not need to be peer reviewed, meaning that they do not need to be read,

evaluated, and approved by other taxonomists before publication. By modern scientific publishing standards, this is considered a relaxed policy, but it allows anyone to describe a new species of organism if he or she can get the description published. The accepted name (in most cases) is the one published first. Because some tarantula species were described more than once, we sometimes see sudden name changes that leave our heads spinning as taxonomists try and decide which name in circulation is tied to what species and which name was published first and is valid. The confusion occurs in part because not all species descriptions are written the same way and the older ones are often infuriatingly sketchy (sometimes not much better than saying "this spider is big and hairy and brown"). In addition, the first preserved specimen used as the basis for the original species description (called the *holotype*) may be lost. When this happens, current researchers can no longer compare the original specimen with new ones to confirm the identity, and they are left with interpreting what may be a vague original description.

All scientific names, when used in their full glory, have the name of the taxonomist who described the species and the year it was described at the end. The scientist's name is in parentheses if the species has been moved to a different genus since the original description. An example is *Ephebopus murinus* (Walckenaer) 1837. This spider, the skeleton tarantula, was first described as *Mygale murina* by the French arachnologist Walckenaer in 1837 and placed into the new genus *Ephebopus* by the French arachnologist Eugene Simon in 1892. Incidentally, it was also described by the English arachnologist Octavius Pickard-Cambridge as *Santaremia pococki* in 1896. This synonomy was later corrected by Simon, who determined that the name *Ephebopus murinus* had precedence over *Santaremia pococki* because it was published first.

Species Accounts

Subfamily Ischnocolinae

Tanzanian dwarf tarantula (*Heterothele villosella*): These are also marketed as the Tanzanian chestnut tarantula. These fascinating little spiders have not received the attention they deserve as representatives of a large and enigmatic group of tarantulas. The tarantula subfamily Ischnocolinae is found throughout most of the world and contains the only tarantulas found in Europe and the Middle East. Most authorities recognize that the Old World and New World ischnocoline tarantulas are distinct from each other but throw up their hands at what the exact relationship is between the two. Most hobbyists will not care one way or another as very few of these tarantulas are sought after by collectors because they tend to be small and drably colored. The Tanzanian dwarf tarantula is only about 1 inch (2.54 cm) in body length and is a master web spinner. It has long spinnerets and will fill a container with webbing. They are easy to keep because they make their own home with silk. I keep mine fairly dry and mist the web weekly to keep them watered. The males are much smaller than the females and have extensive feathering on the legs. They are easy to breed and spin pea-sized egg sacs. The spiderlings will live together on the mother's web for many weeks.

Subfamily Ornithoctoninae

Cobalt blue tarantula (*Haplopelma lividum*): These fierce Asian tarantulas are regularly imported from Thailand and surrounding regions. This is a typical Old World tarantula, short haired and short tempered. Their legs are

A stunning female Cobalt Blue (Haplopelma lividum).

An adult female Thailand black tarantula (Haplopelma minax).

a deep electric blue color in the right light, and they are one of the most colorful of the Asian tarantulas. They also have a pale carapace and a dark gray abdomen with faint striping. These spiders are extremely aggressive, so leave them alone! This hardy obligate burrower from forested regions will build a spectacular turreted burrow in captivity if given the opportunity. A female of mine built a turret several inches high in a tall cage. They emerge from the burrow to sit at the entrance in the evening. If you keep them in a shoe box-style cage, they will quickly line it with silk. I have found balancing moisture levels for these spiders to be a bit tricky. I strike a balance by always having water available but letting the cage dry out periodically. Spiderlings can be even trickier to raise through the early instars. They apparently need both moisture and lots of ventilation. The cobalt blue tarantula is moderately difficult to breed in captivity, but spiderlings are regularly available.

Thailand black tarantula (*Haplopelma minax*): These spiders were imported in large numbers under the trade name Thailand bird-eating spider back in the 1970s. They are sporadically available now as imported adults and captive-bred spiderlings. The coloring of the Thailand black tarantula is not as interesting as the cobalt blue, but this species can be larger (depending on where they were collected). One of the most impressive things about this tarantula is its aggressive nature. This was the first Old World species I ever owned. After years of experience with those gentle North and Central American species, I was absolutely aghast at its threat display. Disturbed Thailand black tarantulas will rise up into a frontal threat posture, toppling over backward, with venom dripping

from their fangs. They may remain in this position for as long as 20 minutes after you have stopped doing whatever you did to get them so annoyed. Their message is clear—back off! Housing for the Thailand black tarantula is the same as for the cobalt blue.

Thailand zebra tarantula (*Haplopelma albostriatum*): This spider is smaller than the cobalt blue and overall dark in color, with pale yellow striping running down the legs. They are sporadically available as both wild-caught and captive-bred stock. They are also from tropical Asia, and their care and housing is the same as for all other *Haplopelma* species.

Asian chevron tarantula (*Cyriopagopus paganus*): This spider has only recently appeared in the pet trade and has done so with a vengeance. It is also marketed as the Thai tiger tarantula or Vietnamese tiger tarantula. The name tiger refers to the striping on the dorsal surface of the abdomen, although it could also refer to its attitude. The genus *Cyriopagopus* is closely related to *Haplopelma,* and we may, in fact, see it transferred to that genus. The Asian chevron tarantula is a larger species than the cobalt blue or Thailand zebra tarantula. It has dark coloring with gray and brown markings on the top of its abdomen. It is a bit leggier than the *Haplopelma* but builds the same type of burrow and can be cared for in the same way. The legginess of the juveniles and adult females is enhanced in the adult males in that have very long bony-looking legs compared with male cobalt blues. Approximately 100 to 200 leggy, black spiderlings hatch from the egg sac.

Subfamly Harpactirinae
Mombassa golden starburst tarantula (*Pterinochilus murinus*): These spiders are the

toughest tarantulas I have ever kept. They will live and breed under the most stringent conditions. They are native to drier regions of east Africa and so depend less on moisture. They are very aggressive and will readily display and bite. Reports describe severe pain and swelling from the bite of these spiders, so take special care when working with them. These are very handsome and have an overall pale-yellowish color (the hue varies depending on where they were collected) with dark markings. The hairs are so short that the tarantulas appear almost hairless. A close relative, called the Usambara orange tarantula from the Usambara Mountain region of Tanzania, is one of the most beautiful of all tarantulas. It can be a stunning reddish gold color. The jury is still out on what species the Usambara orange is, but it may prove to be the same species as the Mombassa golden starburst, just a geographic color variant.

Several species in the genus *Pterinochilus* are in circulation in the pet trade, and they will all flourish in a utilitarian-style housing arrangement. I give them a bit of mulch and a piece of cork bark to attach their copious webbing to and a water dish. They do best if kept on the dry side with good ventilation, but always keep water available. If you are eager to breed a tarantula, I defy you to fail to breed one of these! The males are only slightly smaller than the females and are the same color. Despite their aggressive attitude toward humans, they mate easily. The male can be left in with the female for days or even weeks. The female spins a unique egg sac. Instead of a round sphere, she builds a slinglike, hammock-style egg sac that she lies across and defends vigorously. Out of this sac hatch between 75 and 200 black spiderlings that quickly color up

as they grow. The spiderlings are initially delicate but soon acquire both the attitude and tough constitution of their parents. They also grow quickly. Females may also lay a second clutch without an additional mating (called *double clutching*). So if you breed one of these, be prepared for up to 400 spiderlings!

Straighthorned tarantula (*Ceratogyrus cornuatum*): The straighthorned tarantula is a gray mottled color with darker markings around the eyes. The straighthorned tarantula is also marketed as the greaterhorned tarantula, and the term *baboon spider* is used for all members of this genus. The generic name baboon spider is from the English-speaking peoples of southern Africa. Allegedly, it refers to the similarity of the spiders' legs to baboon fingers. This is a fascinating little genus of seven species of tarantulas that have a hornlike projection on the top of the carapace that can vary in size between a squat button to a distinctly pointed horn, depending on the species. The horn of the straighthorned tarantula is straight and points up. No one has any concrete ideas as to what possible function this horn has. This horn sits on top of the dimple on the center of the carapace (the fovea). When you examine the carapace of the shed skin of any tarantula, you can see that what is a dimple on the outside is the base of a point of cuticle that projects into the cephalothorax on the inside. This point is called an apodeme and is the muscle attachment site for the stomach muscles under the carapace. In the African horned tarantulas the internal apodeme is not a point but a ring-shaped projection. So the appearance of a horn on the carapace may, in fact, relate to the internal anatomy. In other words, maybe the African horned tarantulas did not need a horn,

An adult female Thailand zebra tarantula (**Haplopelma albostriatum**).

An adult female Asian chevron tarantula (**Cyriopagopus paganus**).

but the horn was a by-product of the evolution of the ring. Stranger things have happened in nature!

Curvedhorn tarantula (*Ceratogyrus bechuanicus*): The curvedhorn tarantula is commonly available. Like most other members of the subfamily Harpactirinae, *Ceratogyrus* have very short hairs. They can be maintained in a well-ventilated shoe box type of housing arrangement with dry substrate. Males are similar in size and coloring to the females but usually have a much smaller horn. They are also easy to keep and breed. The females also lay hammock-style egg sacs that produce up to 200 black spiderlings. The horn develops only as the spiders grow. They can sometimes produce a second clutch without mating again.

African redrump tarantula (*Eucratoscelus longiceps*): These spiders are very odd looking because their last pair of legs is covered in long, dense hairs. These hairs are so dense and long they look like they are wearing bell-bottom pants. It is hard to imagine what function the hairs have. However, when the tarantulas are sitting in their burrows head down, all you can see is the dense, backward-pointing brushes of hair on the last two pairs of legs. Perhaps these hairs prevent marauding ants from invading the burrow. They are smaller than the other harpactirines and build a vertical burrow. These spiders are also marketed as Voi redrump baboon spiders. Voi refers to a collecting site in East Africa. Apparently, the adult males are very small when compared with the females, and they have not been bred in captivity very often. I maintain these in gallon plastic jars filled two-thirds of the way up with dry soil and let them dig. If you breed these, you have accomplished something!

Subfamily Eumenophorinae

Cameroon red tarantula (*Hysterocrates gigas*): Cameroon red tarantulas are a rich reddish brown color, fairly hairy looking, with

An adult female Usambara orange tarantula
(Pterinochilus sp.).

An adult female straighthorned tarantula
(Ceratogyrus cornuatum).

stout hind legs. They live in deep burrows in the rain forests of West Africa. They are among the largest of all Old World tarantulas (though not as big as some of the New World giants). Identifying the individual species in this genus is very difficult due to the variable structure of the female genitalia. However, they all look very much alike and are kept the same way. Cameroon red tarantulas are avid burrowers and will construct very deep tunnels if given the chance. These are not a tarantula that can be handled and can be very, very aggressive when disturbed. They need higher humidity than most spiders and must be kept on moist substrate. I use a mixture of peat moss and bark chips. I have noticed that all the tarantulas in the subfamily Eumenophorinae react strongly to light. They do not like it! They will

flee a flashlight beam and I imagine will become stressed out if you do not give them the opportunity to burrow and get into the dark. They will spend most of their time in their burrow but can be seen outside the burrow mouth at night waiting for prey. Since they are such eager burrowers and highly strung, you may not want to acquire one if you are not willing to offer it a chance to burrow.

An adult male straighthorned tarantula
(Ceratogyrus cornuatum). Note the much
smaller horn than the female has.

Reports describe Cameroon red tarantulas in captivity diving into water and capturing fish. I have seen that they will climb into their water dish when disturbed. The genus *Hysterocrates* are easy to breed. The pair can sometimes be left together for days, and the light gray spiderlings are also very tolerant of each other and can be reared together for months. I have had spiderlings live together and feed together for up to six months after hatching.

King baboon tarantula (*Citharischius crawshayi*): The king is one of the most well-known yet poorly understood of the tarantulas. The king baboon is one of the largest of the African tarantulas and extremely aggressive. One unique trait they possess is that the fourth pair of legs are covered in plush, dense hair, making them look very thick. They are a uniform reddish brown color. Like other members of their subfamily, they shun light, and they will eagerly burrow in captivity. They *must* be offered a chance either to burrow in deep, dry soil or to hide under a retreat you provide, such as a piece of cork bark. The king baboon has been a very special challenge for captive breeding because only adult females seem to be exported from Tanzania. Because of this, adult males must be reared out of spiderlings hatching from eggs laid by females imported while gravid. King baboon spiderlings grow slowly and are delicate. Mature male king baboons look very much like adult male Cameroon red tarantulas and are much smaller and more slender than the females (maybe we should be calling them queen baboon tarantulas instead!). Like all the other terrestrial eumenophorine tarantulas, the males lack tibial spurs. Unfortunately, female king baboons in captivity have a nasty habit of eating males rather than mating with them!

Because of this, very few captive breedings of this very special species have occurred. If you keep king baboons, maintain them under ideal conditions and make every attempt to breed them. If you rear out a male, see that it gets a chance to mate. Female king baboons lay an egg sac that they attach to the roof of their retreat. They produce approximately 200 pale red spiderlings.

Togo starburst tarantula (*Heteroscodra maculata*): This tarantula is one of the most evolutionarily enigmatic of tarantula genera, along with its close relative *Stromatopelma*. They are also marketed as the ornamental baboon spider. They have an overall mottled gray color with amazing chalk white markings on the legs. The last pair of legs are thickened near the patella. These are thought to be related to the Cameroon red but are arboreal and lay eggs in sacs they attach to the walls of their retreat. They are native to West Africa, where they live in the crowns of palm trees. I find this spider to be difficult to work with because it is very, very fast and has a reputation for having a nasty bite. I do not recommend this species to anyone who does not have a good deal of tarantula-keeping experience. I chill these spiders in the refrigerator before moving them between cages to slow them down and give me a needed advantage. Their speed, aggressiveness, and allegedly potent venom make them a spider to respect! They will live in an arboreal type of setup and spin a fair amount of silk. I recommend you let them build a retreat to hide in because opening the cage of a startled, darting Togo starburst tarantula is an invitation to disaster. Like other eumenophorine tarantulas, they shun light. The Togo starburst tarantulas breed well in captivity. Males are smaller than the females. Like the adult males of other arboreal tarantula species these males have extensive feathering on their legs that presumably allows them to glide if they fall (or to get away quickly from an unreceptive female!). They produce 100 to 200 black spiderlings.

Red featherleg tarantula (*Stromatopelma calceatum*): This spider is similar in temperament and care to the Togo starburst. However, it is larger in size. Currently two subspecies are in the pet trade: *S. c. calceatum* and *S. c. griseipes*. The first subspecies is the most commonly seen and is a beautiful light orange color with dark markings on the legs that look like spots. The second subspecies is a grayish color overall. The red featherleg is faster and is reputed to have a more poisonous bite than the Togo starburst tarantula, so treat them with a great deal of respect and *be careful*!

Subfamily Selenocosmiinae

Sri Lankan ornamental tarantula (*Poecilotheria fasciata*) **and Indian ornamental tarantula** (*Poecilotheria reglais*): The 13 members of this genus are among the most beautiful and interesting of all tarantulas. These spiders are arboreal and are found only on the island of Sri Lanka and in southern India. Like other Old World tarantulas, ornamentals are fast, high-strung, and have relatively short hair. The markings are a fine pattern of dark gray and greenish brown with light gray. One of the most surprising aspects of these spiders are the bright black and yellow markings on the underside of the forelegs (the femora of the first two pairs of legs). This feature is particularly well developed in the Indian ornamental tarantula (*Poecilotheria regalis*). These brightly marked leg surfaces are exposed during the typical tarantula threat display, making the already awesome display even more striking. These spiders do not spin as much silk as most other arboreal spiders. They may rely more on tree hollows and not have the need for a heavily silked retreat.

Ornamental tarantulas exhibit much greater tolerance for each other than is usual for tarantulas. Reports describe people successfully keeping these spiders in groups of young individuals until the spiders matured. Very young ornamentals have been seen feeding together on prey. This kind of social tolerance is extremely rare in spiders in general and tarantulas in particular. Any attempt to keep these spiders in groups should be viewed as experimental but would be well worth trying if you found yourself with a group of hatchlings and were willing to risk losing a few to cannibalism. Because these spiders come from habitats that can be seasonally very dry, they may aggregate in tree hollows to conserve moisture. Having a group of tarantulas together in an aggregation in a tree hollow could raise the humidity of the air in this kind of confined space and reduce water loss for all the spiders. If the risk of death by dehydration were great enough, it might benefit these normally cannibalistic spiders to tolerate each other and cluster in a moist place.

The Sri Lankan and Indian ornamental tarantulas should be kept as other arboreal species. They are more tolerant of dry conditions than most of the other ornamental tarantulas. I find them among the easier arboreal species to work around. They are much more deliberate in their movements than the African arboreals, for instance. However, they can still be very

A group of Cameroon red spiderlings feeding together on a mouse.

fast. Be aware that reports detail extreme systemic reactions to the bite of these tarantulas! *Do not get bitten! Do not handle these spiders at all!* Breeding ornamental tarantulas is moderately difficult. The male will cohabit with the female for extended periods of time (up to several weeks). I have only once had a female cannibalize a male. After several months, the female will lay her eggs, which will hatch into 75 to 150 large spiderlings.

Trinidad chevron tarantula (*Psalmopoeus cambridgei*) **and Suntiger tarantula** (*Psalmopoeus irminia*): The Trinidad chevron tarantula and closely related suntiger tarantula are among my favorite tarantulas. The Trinidad chevron comes from the Caribbean island of Trinidad just off the northeast coast of Venezuela. Here it can be found in silken retreats along road banks, on houses, and in trees. The Trinidad chevron is an olive green spider with dark stripes on the top of the abdomen. They also have red stripes on the foot segments (metatarsi and tarsi). After a molt, these animals can be the most beautiful moss green. Males are the same general color scheme as the females but are much smaller and have distinct feathering on the legs that allows them to parachute if they fall.

An adult female king baboon tarantula (Citharischius crawshayi).

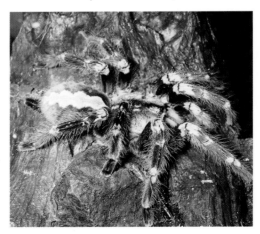

An adult female Sri Lankan ornamental tarantula (Poecilotheria fasciata).

An adult female Togo starburst tarantula (**Heteroscodra maculata**).

An adult female red featherleg tarantula (**Stromatopelma calceatum**).

One of the fascinating things about the genus *Psalmopoeus* is that it is most closely related to the ornamental tarantula genus *Poecilotheria* of the Old World. In fact, when the Trinidad chevron was first described, it was assumed to have come from the East Indies and not the West Indies as was claimed by the collection label. Their overall appearance and demeanor is much more like the short-haired and feisty Old World spiders. The suntiger tarantula is from Venezuela (and is often marketed as the Venezuelan suntiger tarantula). It is very strikingly marked in orangey red and black. It has a black to dark gray background color with vivid red marks on the abdomen where the Trinidad chevron has dark marks on a green background. I have seen suntiger tarantulas living in silken retreats along road banks in southern Venezuela near the Brazilian border. At the time, I was struck with how closely the red marks of the spider matched the red of the earth.

These two spiders readily breed in captivity and have even been hybridized. I never recommend crossing different tarantula species, but Arthur Bordes of Bronx, New York conducted this interesting experiment in the 1970s. The results were instructive as Bordes found that the resulting young were infertile. (These hybrid young were also not as attractive as either parent species.) These two species each lay approximately 100 eggs and will double clutch. Trinidad chevron tarantulas grow quickly, with males maturing in as little as 12 months. Females take a bit longer. These spiders do well in an arboreal setup with a moist substrate for humidity and good ventilation.

Java yellowknee tarantula (*Selenocosmia javanensis*) **Malaysian black velvet tarantula** (*Coremiocnemus* species), and **Mustard tarantula** (*Chilobrachys* species): The Java yellowknee tarantula is one of a large group of brown burrowers from tropical Asia. They are an interesting addition to a tarantula collection because they are representatives of a large subfamily. These are also marketed as the Java birdeater tarantula. Each year, one or two new species of selenocosmine are imported in large enough numbers that they are not very expensive. Recent examples include the Malaysian black-velvet tarantula (*Coremiocnemus* species) and the mustard tarantulas (*Chilobrachys* species). The taxonomy of this group is particularly difficult because they are all dark brown to black, medium-sized tarantulas with no distinctive markings. Both adult males and females tend to have a similar appearance. Adult males do not have tibial spurs, which makes recognizing them a bit trickier. The boundaries between the different genera are determined by the structure of elaborate sound-producing structures between the bases of the front pair of legs and the outside surface of the chelicerae. All these species are active, high-strung, and sensitive to dryness. If maintained in a shoe box setup, they must have water at all times and they will fill the box with silk. If allowed to burrow, they will make a tidy tubular burrow with an inconspicuous entrance.

These genera are moderately difficult to breed and produce between 100 and 200 small spiderlings that are very moisture sensitive. Unfortunately, because they are drab and wild caught specimens that are sold relatively cheaply, they are not being bred with any regularity. This is a shame as they are interesting spiders that will not be on importers' price lists forever.

Subfamily Theraphosinae

Goliath birdeater tarantula (*Theraphosa blondi*): The goliath birdeater is one of the contenders for the World's Largest Spider award. The record for a goliath birdeater is a 12-inch (30 cm) leg span, which is big! They are a rich brown color that can fade to a bright cinnamon color just before a molt. Adult males and females are very similar looking except that the male will have a more slender build and sometimes even a faint iridescent purple coloring on the carapace and femora. This genus is one of very few in the subfamily Theraphosinae in which the males lack tibial spurs. These magnificent spiders are found in the northeastern part of South America: southeastern Venezuela, Guyana, Suriname, French Guiana, and northeastern Brazil. They are found in upland primary rain forest living in distinctive burrows. These burrows are variable in depth but all have a large, open oval burrow mouth with a very faint mat of silk at the opening. In French Guiana, I saw that the burrow mouth was always associated with some habitat structure; a log, root, or rock. They adapt preexisting features in burrow construction.

The goliath birdeater is aggressive, has the ability to emit a loud hissing sound, and has one of the most potent urticating hairs of any tarantula (at least as far as humans are concerned).

They will definitely try to bite. There is no reason to expect that their venom is particularly poisonous, but they are large and are likely to have a lot of it. So being bitten by one would be a bad time to find out you were sensitive to its venom. The goliath birdeater makes its hissing noise during the course of defensive displays by rubbing the forelegs together. The surfaces of the legs, which come into contact, are covered in specially shaped hairs that make the sound. The hairs make the noise in a similar way that Velcro clothing fasteners do. The hairs on the surface of one leg get tangled in the hairs on the opposite leg surface. The goliath birdeating tarantula is definitely not a beginner's spider! Their aggressiveness coupled with their large size and sensitivity to cage conditions make them a handful.

Goliath birdeaters do best in a larger terrarium set up for an opportunistic burrower type of tarantula. I prefer to use an aquarium tank marketed as a 20-gallon (80-L) long, but they will live well and breed in a 10-gallon (40-L) tank. They will usually readily adapt to an artificial burrow. They do not dig a vertical burrow but use a cavelike retreat. Because goliath birdeaters are so heavy bodied and active, I would particularly avoid using a tall tank. If they manage to climb up the sides and fall, the results could be disastrous. These spiders are well worth the effort to give them a well-designed home. They are more moisture dependent than most

*A goliath birdeater tarantula (**Theraphosa blondi**) in front of its burrow. This is an example of an opportunistic burrower. It has dug out a retreat beneath a root in its rain forest home.*

tarantulas in my experience and do poorly in a dry cage. Keep the substrate moist, not wet. I use a mix with lots of peat moss in it. These spiders are found in very rainy areas. The highest population densities I have seen for goliath birdeaters are the Roura Mountains and Kaw Mountains of French Guiana, which are among the rainiest places in the world. Despite their large size, goliath birdeaters mature in about three years. They hatch as very large spiderlings, which gives them a head start on life. Goliath birdeaters will eat a wide variety of prey, including vertebrates (such as small mice and lizards) and nightcrawlers. They have a much larger appetite than most tarantulas from the New World, so feed them well.

The goliath birdeater tarantula is easy to mate in captivity. I have even had males and females drumming to each other from adjacent cages. However, they are moderately difficult to get young from as the females are prone to eating their eggs. I have had good success breeding *Theraphosa* and attribute this success to leaving the females entirely alone during the incubation period. The eggs can take over two months to hatch. Privacy is the key to success: Leave them alone! Keep the cage in a quiet

An adult female Indian ornamental tarantula (**Poecilotheria regalis**).

An adult female Indian ornamental tarantula (**Poecilotheria regalis**).

place, and keep it covered with a dark cloth. If you are looking for a tarantula species to work with that can be dependably bred with care and produce young that will always sell, this is it. Captive breeding will (and should!) be our only source for goliath birdeater tarantulas in the not-too-distant future.

Brazilian salmon tarantula (*Lasiodora parahybana*): The Brazilian salmon is among the largest of the regularly bred tarantulas and does very well in captivity. They are also marketed as Brazilian salmon pink tarantulas. Older adult females are truly impressive in size. They are drab in color, being a grayish black with long pale hairs that may be a pinkish color, but they are handsome spiders nonetheless. They are not handleable and do best in an opportunistic burrower type of cage. They are not as

An adult female Java yellowknee tarantula (**Selenocosmia javanensis**).

An adult female Malaysian blackvelvet tarantula (**Coremiocnemus sp.**).

An adult female goliath birdeater tarantula (**Theraphosa blondi**) *in its rain forest home in French Guiana.*

An adult female suntiger tarantula (**Psalmopoeus irminia**).

moisture dependent as the goliath birdeater tarantula. They are not legally imported as wild-caught stock since they are native to Brazil, a country that prohibits the export of its wildlife. However, they are regularly bred in captivity and can produce over 3,000 eggs in a clutch. No wonder we see them offered for very low prices as captive-bred spiderlings. Males are similar in size and coloration to the females. Females can be aggressive toward the males. So make sure the female is well fed before a mating and also make sure the male can get away in the event she is unimpressed!

Haitian brown tarantula (*Phormictopus cancerides*): The Haitian brown was formerly imported in large numbers and is currently not as readily available. These spiders are found on the island of Hispaniola (Haiti and the Dominican Republic). They have relatives (in the same genus) on Cuba. Unverified published records

and current rumors indicate that *Phormictopus* species tarantulas may, in fact, be found in Puerto Rico, the Bahamas, and even Florida. These allegations have not been confirmed. These spiders are similar in appearance to some of the South American tarantulas in the genus *Pamphobeteus*. Like many *Pamphobeteus*, they are also dark brown in color. Adult males are often covered in beautiful purplish iridescence on the carapace and basal segments of the legs (femora). Haitian browns are a favorite of mine because they were the first of the large, tropical tarantulas I ever kept. They are not generally docile, and I do not recommend handling them. Members of this genus are reported to be wanderers rather than being tied to a particular retreat as are most other tarantulas. Biologists observing tarantulas in the genus *Phormictopus* in Haiti and Cuba report finding them under logs and even boards during the day with no apparent retreat constructed.

These spiders do very well in captivity if given a larger cage and a moist substrate set up as for opportunistic burrowing tarantulas. These spiders are moderately difficult to breed but are frequently offered for sale as captive-bred spiderlings. They produce moderate-sized clutches of large, blue spiderlings. These spiderlings will grow quickly if fed well.

Colombian lesserblack tarantula (*Xenesthis immanis*): The Colombian lesserblack tarantula is one of the handsomest of tarantulas available, being clothed in velvety black hairs with iridescent pink highlights and long red hairs on the abdomen. A freshly molted individual is a stunning sight to behold. Adult males are often spectacularly colored in purple iridescence like the Haitian brown. They are reputed to range from Colombia south to Peru. Despite this wide range, they are rarely imported. These tarantulas unfortunately cannot be handled, the same as most of the large tropical tarantulas. Colombian lesserblack tarantulas are the focus of one interesting study done in Peru because they share their burrows with toads. The researchers proposed that the toad is protected from predation by the tarantula by toxins in their skin and may benefit the spider by eating pestiferous insects too small for the tarantula to catch. They also saw that adult female Colombian lesserblack tarantulas also share their burrows with older offspring.

The Colombian lesserblack tarantula is one of the most difficult to breed of all tarantulas. Furthermore, what clutches they do produce are small. I have found these spiders to be surprisingly slow to shed and grow. They may just have a longer life cycle than any of the other South American giant tarantulas. When they do breed, they produce small numbers of large spiderlings just as goliath birdeater tarantulas and many other South American giants do. I have produced one clutch of these spiders and did so by providing the female with a large, planted terrarium and leaving her entirely alone. In general, the care of these spiders is as for the goliath birdeater.

Chilean common tarantula (*Grammostola rosea*): The Chilean common tarantula is one of the best beginner's spiders. They are a pale tawny background color with varying degrees of pink metallic highlights. The adult males are particularly brightly colored. A geographic color variant of this spider has strong reddish coloring. These were formerly referred to as the Chilean rosehairs. These are wonderful spiders because of their docile, hardy nature and attractive coloring. They are unfortunately undervalued since they are imported in such large numbers from Chile and sold for ridiculously low prices. Because they grow so slowly, this harvest level is not likely to be sustainable at current levels. There is no reason why we cannot support the desire for captive Chilean common tarantulas by breeding them.

A biological oddity of these spiders is that adult male Chilean common tarantulas have been repeatedly reported to molt, which is something *no* adult male spider is supposed to do. In most cases, these males lost the mating organs on the ends of the pedipalps. Why this happened I could not even guess. It is interesting to note that these spiders are very similar in appearance and temperament to a group of tarantulas from the northern limits of the range of tarantulas in the New World: the *Aphonopelma* tarantulas of the United States and Mexico. Both North American *Aphonopelma* and Chilean *Grammostola* are bulky, docile, long-lived, burrowing spiders. These

Tarantulas and the Law

Two regulatory bodies control the trade of live animals in the United States. One is the United States Department of Agriculture, which is not currently concerned with arachnids other than mites and ticks (which might potentially be agricultural pests). The other is the United States Fish and Wildlife Service (USFWS), which regulates the import of all wildlife (live or dead), including tarantulas. At ports of entry, the USFWS officers are on the lookout for the illegal import of species that are listed by CITES (pronounced sy-tees, The Convention on International Trade in Endangered Species of Wild Flora and Fauna) and spiders being illegally exported from countries that protect their spiders. CITES is a treaty organization that recommends protection of plant and animal species based on their risk of extinction due to human exploitation. The CITES Appendix I lists species threatened with extinction. The CITES Appendix II lists species that may become threatened if current rates of exploitation are not regulated. The CITES Appendix III lists all species protected, for whatever reason, in the country of origin. The importation of any listed species requires export permits from the country of origin. Within the United States are endangered and threatened spider species, but none were ever of interest to the animal trade. At this moment (of the arachnids of interest to collectors), only tarantulas in the genus *Brachypelma* and three species of scorpion (in the genus *Pandinus—P. dictator, P. gambiensis,* and *P. imperator*) are listed by CITES in Appendix II. Organisms in this category can be traded only with export permits and CITES documents from the country of origin. The United States Fish and Wildlife Service also requires that you declare the spiders upon entry into the United States. If the country of origin protects their arachnids from export, then you must have export documentation when you arrive at customs. Even if the countries do not specifically protect their spiders (and most do not), most regulate their export very tightly under blanket faunal protection laws! In fact, the country that freely allows the unregulated export of its fauna (even invertebrates!) is very rare.

If you want to import tarantulas from abroad, whether you are receiving them from an exporter or bringing a few back yourself, you need to declare them at the port of entry whether they are CITES listed or not. In addition, you will need a document from the country of origin saying exporting the spiders is OK. Be prepared to work with officials who may not be well versed in the laws regulating the importation of live arachnids. Obviously, it is not something that they deal with every day! Know the law before you leave the country. I have found customs officials to be genuinely curious about the spiders. It must be a wonderful break from the tedium of poking through the dirty laundry of returning tourists to see some big, hairy spiders!

When you pack the spiders in the country of origin, be sure that no vegetative debris or soil is in the container. The USDA closely controls any import of plants or dirt since these could harbor crop pests. Pack the tarantulas in snug boxes with moist paper towel padding to protect the spider and provide moisture.

An adult female Brazilian salmon tarantula (**Lasiodora parahybana**) *with her egg sac.*

An adult male Haitian brown tarantula (**Phormictopus cancerides**).

traits may be associated with the ability to colonize more seasonal climates, such as Chile and the American Southwest.

Chilean common tarantulas can be maintained in simple caging with a sandy substrate, a cork bark retreat, and a water dish. They are more resistant to dry conditions than most tarantulas and do not need any special attention paid to humidity. They will attempt to dig, moving the substrate around the cage, but are rarely successful in constructing a burrow even if you give them a deep enough substrate. You may have success getting them to adapt an artificial burrow. They have been bred and produce large clutches. Because the mass exportation of this species from Chile will not continue forever (nor should it), efforts to breed them should increase.

Ecuadorian brownvelvet tarantula (*Megaphobema velvetosoma*): These spiders are similar to goliath birdeaters in general body shape and

behavior except for the thickened patellae and tibiae on the last pair of legs. Also, adult males and females are very similar in appearance. However, they are about half the size of the goliath birdeater. They are from the Amazon region of Ecuador where they live in burrows. These spiders are interesting in that they have a distinctive mating behavior. Receptive females have a dramatic drumming display they perform for courting males. It is a loud and emphatic "Yes!" When they mate, the males almost flip the female over backward, so extreme is the flexion of her body during the actual mating.

Ecuadorian brownvelvet tarantulas can be kept like goliath birdeater tarantulas. They are too active and aggressive to handle.

Colombian giant tarantula (*Megaphobema robustum*): These are among the most handsomely marked of all tarantulas, being dark bodied and having orange legs. Despite their name, these spiders are not as nearly as large

An adult female Ecuadorian brownvelvet tarantula (Megaphobema velvetosoma).

An adult female Colombian giant tarantula (Megaphobema robustum).

as the goliath birdeater tarantula. They are also marketed as Colombian redleg tarantulas. They are a typical South American opportunistic burrower: They like their habitat moist and will use an artificial retreat. They are very rarely exported from Colombia and also rarely bred. Imported spiders and captive-bred spiderlings are occasionally offered for sale.

Greenbottle blue tarantula (*Chromatopelma cyaneopubescens*): This spider was a sensation when it was first imported from Venezuela because of its stunning coloration. It is the only tarantula species I know of in which the subadults and adults of both sexes are entirely iridescent in coloration. The whole body, apart from the bright orange abdomen, is a stunning midnight blue shading into green around the

front of the body. They are modest-sized tarantulas and are oddities for reasons other than their stunning coloration. Currently, only one species is in the genus *Chromatopelma*, and its closest relatives are in the genus *Cyclosternum*. *Cyclosternum* species tarantulas are very sensitive to moisture. However, the greenbottle blue is an arid-adapted spider, and older juveniles and adults need relatively dry conditions. Only the youngest spiderlings need to be kept moist. They live in arid scrublands in northern

A pair of Bolivian steelyblue tarantulas (Pampobeteus antinous) *courting. The male is in the front.*

Venezuela where the adults spin silken retreats under debris on the ground. You can maintain these spiders the same as the genus *Pterinochilus*: dry. Not only that, but the juveniles can be kept on the dry side as well.

The greenbottle blue has a reputation for being difficult to breed because they are a bit highly strung and may mate only when left alone. They are best paired by placing the female's cage into a large container and leaving the male loose in the larger enclosure. This way he can get away if things go wrong!

Bolivian steelyblue tarantula (*Pamphobeteus antinous*): This spider is a member of a fairly large South American genus that contains some of the most colorful of the New World tarantulas. Despite being regularly imported and being considered desirable captives, *Pamphobeteus* species tarantulas are very rarely bred. The Bolivian steelyblue is my favorite *Pamphobeteus* because of its coloring, which is similar to that of the Colombian lesserblack except that the iridescent highlights are a deep blue. Most other *Pamphobeteus* species tarantulas are a dark brown color, but all are known for their often spectacular iridescent highlights. This species apparently includes two different populations that differ in size. Spiders imported from the Bolivian populations are said to be larger than those from the Peruvian populations.

Pamphobeteus species tarantulas are all opportunistic burrowers and need high humidity. Most species are too fast and high-strung to be safely handled. I would consider the Bolivian steelyblue to be difficult to breed based on the lack of captive-bred spiderlings on the market and my own experiences. The males are extremely nervous during courtship, and mating takes place very quickly. I have succeeded in getting egg sacs from several females, but they were all infertile. Others have had similar experiences with them.

Brazilian whiteknee tarantula (*Acanthoscurria geniculata*): This spider caused a sensation when it came onto the U.S. market in 1998 because it is arguably one of the most spectacularly marked of all tarantulas. The markings are a stunning dark gray to black background color with bright white leg bands. This spider is also marketed as the giant whiteknee tarantula. This species is native to Brazil. Captive stocks are reportedly descended from egg sacs and spiders smuggled out of Brazil into Germany. The genus *Acanthoscurria* is one of the most species-rich tarantula genera in the world at approximately 38 species. This could mean that systematic revision will result in breaking this genus into a group of smaller genera. Most *Acanthoscurria* are small, stocky, and drably colored. The Brazilian black and white is among the larger and perhaps the most strikingly colored.

The Brazilian whiteknee tarantula should be housed as other South American opportunistic burrowers. Give them room, an artificial retreat, and keep them on the dry side. Thankfully, they are proving to be only moderately difficult to breed, so captive populations will likely prove self-sustaining. They produce large clutches (around 1,000) of tiny spiderlings. These are dark and unmarked when very young but color up quickly and grow fast.

Costa Rican zebra tarantula (*Aphonopelma seemani*): The Costa Rican zebra is one of the best of the pet tarantulas. They are also marketed as the stripeknee tarantula. They combine striking markings with hardiness to make them one of the better beginner's spiders.

A Mexican blond tarantula (Aphonopelma chalcodes) *sits by its burrow in the Sonoran desert. This is an example of an obligate burrower. Because their burrow requirements are so unique, these tarantulas must dig their own rather than use a pre-existing burrow.*

Unfortunately, many individuals are too skittish to handle safely. The Costa Rican zebra is a light to dark gray color with cream-colored stripes running down the legs. Two color morphs of the Costa Rican zebra are said to exist, one bluer than the other. These tarantulas are common burrowers in grassland areas of Costa Rica and other countries in Central America. They are sporadically imported and are also available as captive-bred spiderlings. Adult males are darker than the females in color. They dig vertical burrows in the wild and can be induced to take to artificial burrows in captivity. The life cycle of these spiders is short for the genus, with males maturing in two to three years (compared with males of some more northerly species maturing in nine years).

Costa Rican zebra tarantulas tolerate a variety of conditions in captivity. They can be maintained as an obligate burrower tarantula. You are likely to have greater success in getting them to accept an artificial burrow than inducing them to dig their own from scratch.

Trinidad olive tarantula (*Hapalopus incei*): This spider is a small tarantula with attributes that make it an interesting addition to a collection. They are among the smaller tarantulas available to hobbyists, being only about 2 inches (approximately 5 cm) in body length. This species has been a taxonomic puzzle, having been placed both in the subfamilies Ischnocolinae and Theraphosinae. They lack urticating hairs, which argues against them being theraphosines, but do have other attributes that they share with the Theraphosinae. They are an attractive greenish brown color with a dorsal abdominal pattern. In captivity, they spin lots of silk. In the wild in Trinidad, they can be found under rocks and on road banks where they make a retreat by filling in crevices with silk within which they have a tubular retreat. The adult males are very small. Spiderlings of this species are small and are among the oddest-looking tarantula spiderlings in that they have a black body with pale legs. Keep them moist with attachment sites for their copious silk.

Andean stripeleg tarantula (*Lasiodorides striatus*): This spider is one of those species to show up only recently in shipments from Peru. The genus is also very recently described, although the spider was known for a time as *Pamphobeteus wallacei*. They are leggy and have a dark gray color fading out to brown between molts, with longitudinal leg striping. They are much larger than the similar-looking

An adult female Brazilian whiteknee tarantula (**Acanthoscurria geniculata**).

An adult female Trinidad olive tarantula (**Hapalopus incei**).

Costa Rican zebra tarantula, with some females reaching a 7.5-inch (over 18 cm) leg span. This species is reputed to be easy to breed in captivity, and the egg sacs contain 350 to 500 spiderlings. Spiderlings grow moderately quickly. This is a less-aggressive but active species that needs the standard housing for opportunistic burrowers. They don't need very moist conditions and will do well with moderate humidity. A closely related species is called the Peruvian blond

tarantula (*L. polycuspulatus*), which is smaller, shaggier and a light brown color overall.

Mexican blond tarantula (*Aphonopelma chalcodes*): The Mexican blond tarantula is one of the two most attractive tarantulas found in the United States (despite the name). Immatures and adult females are a pale, tawny color, with dark basal leg segments (the femora). Adult males are slate blue with a pale carapace and reddish abdomen. The sexually mature Mexican blond males and females have to be one of the most differently marked (sexually dimorphic) of any adult tarantulas. The Mexican blond tarantula is found in the Sonoran Desert of southern Arizona and northern Mexico. It used to be much more commonly seen in

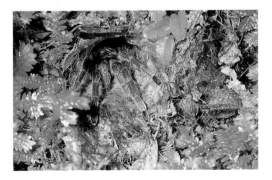

The retreat of a Trinidad olive tarantula on a road bank in the Northern Range of Trinidad. Note the legs of the spider visible in the entrance.

An adult female Andean stripeleg tarantula
(Lasiodorides striatus).

An adult female Mexican blond tarantula
(Aphonopelma chalcodes).

the pet trade in the United States, and it was formerly referred to as the Arizona blond or palomino tarantula.

The first tarantulas I ever saw in the wild were Mexican blond tarantulas in the vicinity of Tucson. These spiders dig deep, cylindrical burrows straight down into the hard, gravelly soil. These burrows are distinctive in the desert, a place with lots of burrowing animals. The mouth is almost perfectly round with a fine mat of silk around the edge. During the day, the spiders cover the opening with a fine mesh of silk. This veil may limit airflow and thus evaporative water loss in a place where water is hard to come by. Burrows can be over 2 feet (60 cm) deep. Research has shown that the temperatures found at the bottom of the burrow are very mild compared with the surface. These are among the most seasonal of the tarantulas since they live in a seasonal environment. Mexican blond tarantulas in Arizona will plug their

burrows for six months of the year, from October to May. Adult males are seen in large numbers crossing highways during July and August when they are searching for females. I have never seen hatchling Mexican blond tarantulas in the wild, but I have heard of spiderlings being found living under dead and decaying cacti. They may live like this until they are large and strong enough to dig their own burrow in the hard desert soil. The longest life cycles of all tarantulas are recorded for North American species. The Mexican blond tarantula is likely to follow this model and take 9 to 10 years to mature. Adult females can live an additional 20 years or more, with adult males usually living only through the summer of their maturity.

Mexican blond tarantulas are extremely hardy captives. They will do fine in a simple cage with a sandy substrate. They are very docile and can usually be freely handled. An additional advantage to owning the blond tarantula is that their urticating hairs are not usually irritating to humans. Research suggests that the hairs are shaped to offer defense against predation by grasshopper mice. There is scarcely a more benign tarantula then these.

Breeding in captivity has proven tricky, perhaps due to the seasonal environment Mexican blond tarantulas come from. Important cues of temperature or light may be missing in captivity. Mexican blond tarantulas will eat a variety of insect prey. These spiders are capable of prodigious feats of fasting and are known to have gone over two years without food. They have such low metabolisms, and can store so much fat in their abdomens, that they often go off feed for months on end, particularly during the winter months.

Most of what I said about the management of the Mexican blond tarantula is applicable to any of the other *Aphonopelma* species tarantulas found in the United States. Very few of the approximately 30+ species of *Aphonopelma* native to the United States find their way into the pet trade. These spiders are rarely offered for sale since most are too drab in coloration to be considered desirable by a majority of collectors. An exception is the beautifully marked Rio Grande gold tarantula (*Aphonopelma moderatum*) from southern Texas. In addition, the Texas tan tarantula (*Aphonopelma anax*) is a large, feisty captive that is handsome and occasionally bred and offered for sale as spiderlings. Interestingly, the Texas tan tarantula grows much more quickly than the Mexican blond. This may occur because the Texas tan tarantula lives in much moister, prey-rich habitats than the Mexican blond tarantula inhabits in the Sonoran Desert; its life cycle is a bit faster, from hatching to maturity.

If you want to see tarantulas in the wild in the United States, you need to go west. American tarantulas are distributed from central Missouri across to northern California and south to the Mexican border. In the eastern and northern parts of their range, they are found in drier habitats, such as the cedar barrens of Arkansas and grasslands of Kansas and Missouri. In California, they are widely distributed inland from the coast. There are no confirmed records of naturally occurring tarantulas from east of the Mississippi River or north of the Missouri River. This may at first seem surprising, given that some states seem perfect for tarantulas, such as Florida. However, tarantulas are not great travelers, and Old Man River may be a real barrier to their movement east. Rivers are well known to define the limits of species distributions, including spiders. An exception to this rule is the population of Mexican redrump tarantulas in east central Florida (see the species account).

Locating tarantula burrows takes either very exact location information or persistence. In the western states, I have found that tarantula burrows are mostly found on gently sloping ground. Dry streambeds will not do. I have also noticed that you almost never find just one. Because tarantulas are not very good travelers, they rarely wander far from their mother's burrow before settling down on their own. This means that you typically find tarantula burrows in local aggregations (sometimes called *colonies*). Several alternative methods can be used to collect tarantulas from their burrows. Flushing tarantulas from their burrow is possible with water. This trick works well only if you have not made the tarantula aware of your presence by moving noisily around the burrow. If you lose the element of surprise, the spider will sit tight, even under water. This is not a great hardship for a spider in the desert! You can also dig up the spider, which can be hard going in the gravelly soils in some areas. At night, it is not too hard to tease them out of their burrows with a twig or blade of grass, fooling them into thinking it is a struggling insect. If you find a population in an area safe from development, please resist the temptation to collect all the specimens in your enthusiasm, as these spiders have such a long life cycle wiping out the local population for a long time, if not forever, would be possible. A good rule is never to take more than several (certainly never more than 10 percent of the population) from a given site.

Mexican redknee tarantula (*Brachypelma smithi*): The Mexican redknee tarantula is generally considered to be the most desirable of all the pet tarantulas. The beauty and docility of the redknee is legendary. This species, more than any other, is responsible for the advent of tarantula keeping in the United States. A healthy, recently molted redknee is strikingly marked in bright shades of orange and velvet black. Adult males have similar coloring as the females. During the 1970s, Mexican redknees were imported in vast numbers from their native haunts in the Pacific states of Mexico (in the vicinity of Acapulco). Unfortunately, the Mexican redknee has a relatively long life cycle (taking five to seven years to mature) and it was felt that the demand for the pet trade began to overtake its reproductive rate. The spiders were being overexploited, and attempts were made to regulate the import of wild-caught redknees.

At the time of writing, the Mexican redknee tarantula (and all members of the genus

Brachypelma) are listed on CITES Appendix II. Because Mexico does not currently permit the export of its CITES-listed wildlife, dealing in wild-caught Mexican tarantulas is illegal. Fortunately for tarantula aficionados, captive breeding has been increasingly successful. Not only are Mexican redknees reproducing in captivity, they are very productive, producing up to 1,000 spiderlings at a time! So, while you might view the legality of any adult or subadult redknees offered for sale with skepticism, captive-bred spiderlings are regularly available. The life cycle is long, but hatchlings begin to acquire the coloration of adults at the end of their first year. Buying a hatchling tarantula that will not mature for years may seem like a long time to wait, but you will have the satisfaction of knowing you are not contributing to the decline of a vulnerable species and will have a pet that you can enjoy for many years.

Mexican redknees are hardy captives that can be kept in a variety of cages. You can go for simplicity or attempt to induce your spider to adopt an artificial burrow. They use an opportunistic burrower type of retreat and a sandy substratum. Older individuals can tolerate relatively dry conditions, and attention to humidity is important only for very young specimens (see the chapter about rearing spiderlings). Mexican redknees do have urticating hairs that cause a severe reaction in some people, so take care when handling them. Rinse your hands after handling a redknee to remove any stray hairs.

Adult male Mexican redknee tarantulas look very similar to the females. They are fairly easy to pair, but getting eggs from the females is a bit harder. They will apparently breed in simple housing with a shelter. The moderate difficulty

in breeding these spiders is offset by their large clutch sizes. Spiderlings are very small and pale. They need moist conditions. Small Mexican redknees get very, very fat between molts. This is just their growth strategy. So, while over-feeding adults is a bad idea, if you want your spiderlings to grow quickly, feed them heavily, even when they look like they might pop.

An adult female Rio Grande gold tarantula (**Aphonopelma moderatum**).

An adult female Mexican redrump tarantula (**Brachypelma vagans**) *with her egg sac. This female was photographed in the wild in central Florida.*

Mexican redleg tarantula (*Brachypelma emilia*): Mexican redlegs are a more subtly colored relative of the redknee. They are also marketed as painted tarantulas. Redlegs are known to be even more docile than redknees. They do not get as large as the redknee and have a striking dark triangular marking on the carapace that is unmistakable. This species is also native to western Mexico and is able to tolerate drier conditions. Maintain the redleg the same way as the redknee.

Several other species are in the *Brachypelma smithi* species group, all stunningly marked in black and red. These spiders are all protected by the laws of Mexico from export but are being bred in captivity. All these spiders have similar housing requirements as the Mexican redknee.

Mexican redrump tarantula (*Brachypelma vagans*): The redrump tarantula is a very hand-some spider that is well established in captivity due to the relative ease of captive propagation. Mexican redrump tarantulas look nothing like the Mexican redknee and redleg tarantulas, being a black to dark gray color with long red hairs on the abdomen. They are at least as large as the Mexican redknee. These spiders are native to tropical areas of southern Mexico. The docility of the Mexican redrump is variable, but some individuals can be handled. They need a more tropical environment than the Mexican redknee and redleg tarantulas. They will do well with a moist substrate and an artificial burrow.

The Mexican redrump is the first tarantula known to have been introduced into a new region by people. In 1997, a colony of these spiders was discovered in a citrus grove approximately 30 miles (48 km) west of Fort Pierce, Florida. The State of Florida responded as they must when confronted by yet another exotic species within its boundaries by trying very hard to exterminate the tarantulas. However, despite some intensive insecticide applications, the tarantulas persist. I went to the site in 1999 and saw eight tarantulas. One female I collected had an egg sac. While it was very exciting to collect the tarantulas, it was also troubling to see yet another exotic species in the wild in Florida, a state already overrun with exotic plants and animals. While the Mexican redrump is unlikely to do any harm to the Florida environment because they are slow breeding and slow moving, some exotic species have not been so benign. Rumors suggest that these spiders were intentionally introduced into the citrus groves as spiderlings hatching from eggs laid by females imported from Mexico for the pet trade in the 1970s.

Curlyhair tarantula (*Brachypelma albopilosum*): The curlyhair was formerly imported in great numbers from Honduras. These are one of the most unique-looking of all tarantulas as they have a dark brown background color with longer, lighter-colored hairs all over the body. The length and curliness of these hairs is extreme. These spiders are still occasionally imported from Central America and are also regularly bred. They do best in a tropical environment, with conditions similar to those for the Mexican redrump. They are moderately easy to breed. The spiderlings grow fast, with males maturing in as little as two years. They produce

A pinktoe tarantula (Avicularia sp.) on the underside of a palm leaf in French Guiana.

large clutches of small spiderlings. I had a small female produce over 800 spiderlings, which is a very large clutch by any standards.

Subfamily Aviculariinae

Pinktoe tarantulas (*Avicularia species*): *Avicularia* is the most widespread tarantula genus in the New World, being found from Puerto Rico to southern Bolivia. Approximately 20 species are described. Almost all species have pink (or light) marks on the toes (ends of the tarsi), are very fuzzy looking, and are generally dark in color. They undergo one of the most extreme color transformations of any tarantula when they mature. Immatures are often more strikingly marked than the adults, with bold banding patterns on the top of the abdomen. Very young spiderlings can have very pale legs and dark feet, almost a reverse color scheme to that of the adults. As noted in the chapter Understanding Tarantulas, the genus *Avicularia* has the distinction of being the first of the tarantulas described by science. They are also one of the only arboreal tarantulas that possess urticating hairs. These hairs are unique in their structure among all tarantulas. Five of the six described types of urticating hairs attach to the spider's body by a stalk on the opposite end of the hair from the penetrating end. For pinktoes, the urticating hair is attached to the cuticle of the spider by a stalk on the hair near (but not at) the piercing end.

Pinktoe tarantulas can be abundant in parts of their range. They are the only tarantula I know that may benefit from human intrusion into their habitats. I have seen them in very high densities in and around human habitations in French Guiana. They are commonly seen in the eaves of houses, in shrubs, and on trees planted around towns. They are almost invariably seen in pineapple plants. The factors that probably contribute to the success of the pinktoe are their ability to tolerate fluctuating humidity (as they construct a very heavy silk retreat), their urticating hairs, and their arboreal habit (which facilitates retreat placement around human habitation). Pinktoes have been imported in large numbers from Peru and Guyana in recent years. Take care when you purchase a pinktoe to note the country of origin or scientific name since identifying the species can be very difficult or even impossible. They mature in two to three years. They are usually docile and can be handled. However, like the redknee, watch for the urticating hairs that are employed by the spider in a very different way. When handling a pinktoe, watch out for it raising and dipping its abdomen with its legs spread. It is trying to rub some of its urticating hairs onto you.

Pinktoe tarantulas are all arboreal and colonize human structures and vegetation rather than earth banks like the Trinidad chevron tarantula. They will do well in an arboreal setup. Pinktoes have been reported to be able to live in colony cages, like the ornamental tarantulas. Keepers have reported short-term success keeping them in groups, although they are not as sociable as the ornamental tarantulas. Their docility also makes pairing them easier, and you can leave the males in with the females for weeks. Pinktoes are generally easy to breed and produce approximately 50 to 200 young. Raising very young pinktoe spiderlings is a bit tricky since they need both good ventilation and moist conditions. Because of this, they need closer attention than many tarantula spiderlings.

Antilles pinktoe tarantula (*Avicularia versicolor*): This species is one of the all-time favorites of collectors due to its stunning coloration. The metallic shades of green, blue, purple, and pink are absolutely unreal. These spiders are native to the Caribbean islands of Martinique, Guadeloupe, and Dominica. They are very rarely exported from the French island of Martinique. However, they do breed in captivity. We can hope to continue to be able to keep them as captive-bred stock. Adult males and females are similar in appearance, and the Antilles pinktoe is one of the smaller *Avicularia* species tarantulas. Spiderlings are a beautiful blue and black coloration and get the adult color pattern only when they are well grown.

Trinidad mahogany tarantulas (*Tapinauchenius plumipes*): Trinidad mahogany tarantulas are related to pinktoe tarantulas and look like pinktoes with a crew cut. They lack the urticating hairs of the pinktoes. They are a greenish brown color and have pale toes (tarsi). Some populations in the Guiana region of

South America have a purplish sheen, and they have been referred to as *Tapinauchenius purpureaus*. Whether these purple spiders are actually a distinct species from *T. plumipes* is not clear, but they are certainly worth maintaining as a separate bloodline in captivity.

These spiders are small arboreal spiders with a slightly more nervous disposition than the pinktoes. They are rarely imported but are frequently offered for sale by breeders, indicating the ease with which they may be bred in captivity. These are hardy captives that can be maintained the same as pinktoes. One thing unique about the genus *Tapinauchenius* is how fast they will grow. They may be the fastest growing of all tarantulas. Not only do they feed voraciously and shed quickly, they also come through a molt with tiny abdomens. They do not hold anything back in their race to mature! Feed these heavily, and stand back!

Orange treespider tarantula (*Tapinauchenius gigas*): This tarantula is one of my personal favorites because it is a beautiful pinkish red color. It is a native of French Guiana and can be found living in trees in forested areas. It is a similar size to the Trinidad mahogany and can be maintained in the same way. I have several times had small female orange treespiders lay eggs without having mated. Because of their small size, I thought they were immature and had not gotten them a male and one day found them with eggs. Needless to say, these eggs did not hatch. Like the Trinidad mahogany, this spider also grows very fast.

Skeleton tarantula (*Ephebopus murinus*): Skeleton tarantulas are so-called due to lengthwise striping on the legs, which someone

evidently thought made them look like a spider in a skeleton Halloween suit. They have a similar pattern of markings as the Costa Rican zebra tarantula but are even more strikingly marked. Freshly molted individuals have jet-black legs with canary yellow stripes running the length of the outer segments (patellae, tibiae, and metatarsi) and are a stunning sight. The carapace is light brown, the abdomen dark. The skeleton tarantula is a member of a unique genus of tarantulas that carry their urticating hairs on their pedipalps. The urticating hairs are located on the inside surfaces of the long segment (femora), and they shed these by rubbing these hair-bearing surfaces against the bases of their mouth parts (the chelicerae). Skeleton tarantulas are obligate burrowers from French Guiana and northeastern Brazil. They are very aggressive and reminiscent of the Thailand black tarantula in habits and temperament. I have seen them in high densities on road banks in French Guiana.

Skeleton tarantulas are imported sporadically and have been bred only rarely. Their striking markings make them well worth acquiring. A second species in the same genus in the pet trade is called the redskeleton tarantula (*E. rufescens*) that is reportedly easier to breed than the skeleton. The redskeleton tarantula is an overall reddish brown color. They are too aggressive to be handled. Skeleton tarantulas should be maintained in tanks set up for obligate burrowers with attention paid to humidity. A deep peaty mix with bark chips for structure will do. They will spin a large silken funnel at the burrow mouth and sit there at night waiting for prey.

BREEDING TARANTULAS

Breeding any wild creature in captivity can be an extremely exciting experience but it presents many problems that simple pet keeping does not. Bringing together an adult pair of tarantulas, having a successful mating, getting the female through the incubation period, and separating and rearing the spiderlings all present challenges.

Sex and the Single Tarantula

The cannibalistic tendencies of tarantulas are generally overrated, and I have rarely lost a male to a hungry female. Sexual cannibalism (as it is called) is only common among spider species in which the female is much larger than the male. As it turns out, the trickiest part of the whole process is getting a female tarantula to lay a sound egg sac and care for it. Many decide to eat the eggs rather than care for it. If you are willing to go through the process and perhaps end up with hundreds of hungry spiderlings that all need separate housing and small prey items, here is how to get started.

Getting a Pair

There are two major problems preventing you from putting together an adult pair of tarantulas:

A pair of goliath birdeater tarantulas about to mate. The male is in the front.

1. Correctly identifying tarantulas to species can be a challenge, and

2. Most adult male tarantulas do not live very long.

The first problem means that you have to be careful that you have tarantulas of the same species, or a dead male could be the result. The second problem means that adult males are generally in shorter supply than adult females. Once you learn to recognize adult males you will notice that you rarely see them for sale. You are not likely to be able to find a sexual pair of adult tarantulas in a pet store but it may be that your pet shop owner could find an adult wild-caught pair from a wholesale dealer, although it is unlikely. An alternative to buying adults is to acquire several immatures from the same source of the same type and wait for males and females to mature. If the tarantulas came into the country in the same shipment and look alike as immatures, they may in fact be the same species. However, just to cloud the issue, many tarantula species are sexually dimorphic as adults. This means that adult males and females do not look very much alike. This is especially true of burrowing spiders from the American Southwest. Females will be some shade of brown, whereas the males may be strikingly marked in steel blue and red. If you have a group of spiders you are raising from the same clutch bred in captivity, you will not be able to mate brothers and sisters because the males mature at an earlier age than females, and die of old age before the females are mature. Anyway, inbreeding is a poor management decision. Overall, the best choice is to keep tarantulas bred in captivity and acquire individuals in successive years. The most widely kept types are fairly easy to identify and breeders keep track of what they have. But never guess at identification. Putting tarantulas of different species together to breed will increase the chance the female will see her suitor as a meal and not a mate.

Hybridizing

Some tarantula breeders have hybridized tarantula species in the genera *Brachypelma* and *Poecilotheria*. This is an extremely bad idea because we are entirely dependent on captive breeding to be able to keep these species legally. If we allow hybridizing to continue unchecked we will soon have an array of unidentifiable hybrid spiders to keep. Ultimately, creating hybrids does not lead to something new to keep and breed;it leads to the loss of the parental species in captivity. Some people justify hybridizing by arguing that in some cases hybrids occur in the wild. Yes, this may be true, but such "hybrid zones" (as they are called by biologists) are usually found in a very small part of the two parent species' range where they overlap. In captivity we have far fewer tarantulas to breed from than are found in nature and so a little hybridizing can do much more damage to captive gene pools. Given there are over 850 tarantula species out there, and new species being imported all the time, we shouldn't need to engage in wasteful breeding practices like hybridizing to produce novelty. If you are tired of the "same old species," breed something new. While some of these hybrids may be interesting to look at, they are

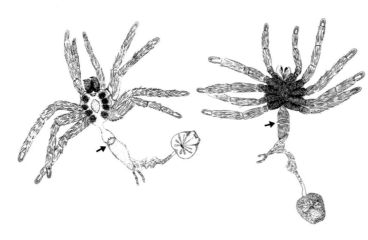

One of the best ways to determine if you have an adult female tarantula is to examine a shed skin. Because tarantulas shed the lining of their genitalia with their skin you can examine the stage of development of the spermatheca by looking at the molt. On the right hand drawing the arrow is pointing to the epigastric furrow viewed externally. On the left hand drawing you can see the same site viewed internally, with the two spermathecae (appearing as the two halves of an "M") visible.

Shipping Tarantulas

Tarantulas ship amazingly well using commercial overnight express delivery services. Because they have such low metabolisms and do not require lots of fresh air, you can pack them snugly inside a box, send them off overnight express, and expect them to arrive alive. The key to success in shipping spiders is to pack them snugly. It is absolutely crucial that the spider cannot be slammed against the sides of the shipping container when the box is in transit. This kind of physical trauma is the primary killer of tarantulas being shipped. Packing tarantulas takes steady nerves and swift hands because you need to pack them tight. Convincing a large spider to get into a small container can be tricky! I use plastic vials or boxes that I line with paper towels. You need to have a small enough container and enough padding that the spider can barely move at all. Then this inner container is packed with lots of padding and placed into a sturdy cardboard box or, best of all, a foam-lined shipping box.

The spider must not be exposed to low temperatures (below 50°F or 10°C). If you are shipping in cooler weather, you can include a chemical hand warmer in the outer box. These hand warmers are sold in sporting goods stores for people engaged in winter sports to warm their hands and feet. These chemical packs are very safe and generate heat by using the chemical reaction of rusting iron. It is surprising that this would work, but all the pouches contain is sawdust, salt, iron filings, and water. When you cut the outer packet open, oxygen can get in that allows the iron to rust. The packets can get very warm to the touch. Because this reaction consumes oxygen (which the spiders also need), you may want to make sure you put a hole or two into the outer box. Before shipping, make sure the carrier will accept live spiders. You cannot get a guarantee of live arrival unless you use air cargo carriers. This is safer for the spiders, particularly in the winter months, but means a trip to the airport.

rarely as attractively marked as the parent species. So don't waste important breeding opportunities creating dead-end hybrids and breed only within species!

Males in the Mail

A good way to get a suitable male for your female tarantula is to arrange to get one on breeding loan from another hobbyist. The usual agreement is to share any offspring produced 50:50. This can work out great and I have received, paired, and then sent on many

males to other breeders. I have had a couple of male tarantulas stop off to meet my females before continuing on a nation-wide tour! While it is true that for tarantulas adult males are the traveling sex, these jet-setting studs are breaking all previous records for tarantula paternity. As we inevitably turn to breeding many species in captivity as our only source for spiders, it is more and more important that you make any adult males you have available for breeding. Just remember, there are no guarantees! Males do get eaten by females

without mating; females may never lay eggs or eat the eggs before hatching. Most breeding loans come to nothing, but when they do work, you may be the happy recipient of hundreds of spiderlings for very little work, just the shipping charges and a bit of luck.

Consenting Adults?

The biggest pitfall in tarantula breeding is the condition of the female. She not only has to be sexually mature, but she has to be in good physical condition and "happy." By happy I mean that she has to be apparently well adjusted to captive conditions. There should be no symptoms of poor acclimatization, such as pacing, excessive digging, bald abdomen, etc. The female should have been fed all she wants and not approaching a molt. You have two

The Costa Rican zebra tarantula (**Aphonopelma seemani**) *is commonly available as both wild-caught imports from Central America and as captive-bred spiderlings.*

choices when it comes to telling if a female is adult: you can ask the male (see section on "Tarantula Sex," page 9), or you can check for fully developed reproductive organs.

Reproductive Organs

The part you examine consists of the epigastric furrow and the spermatheca. The spermatheca is the part of the reproductive tract that stores sperm. These only become fully developed at maturity. If you kept the last shed skin for the spider, you can find these structures, as the tarantula sheds the old lining of the epigastric furrow and spermatheca with her old cuticle. You can examine the freshly shed skin (when it is still moist), or soften a dried molt by soaking it in water with a little dish detergent in it. Spread the skin of the abdomen out on a flat surface. Be sure to use rubber gloves if this is a tarantula with urticating hairs! You can see the pale-colored linings of the book lungs and, in between the book lungs, the epigastric furrow and the spermatheca. The epigastric furrow will look like a pocket that goes from back to front and it should be almost half as deep as it is wide. Attached to this (in some species) will be small, paired spermathecae. These will vary in shape depending on the species. In immatures there will be a small fold where the epigastric furrow is, but it will not be anywhere as deep as the mature female's.

Signals

When I said "ask the male," I was not being flippant, I mean that you can use the male's behavior as a cue as males know before they even get near the female if she is ready to mate, based on her pheromone. Spiders, like many invertebrates, rely on a wide range of chemical signals to exchange information. Female spiders have a specific chemical signal they secrete in their silk to let the male know they are ready. Some spiders have even been shown to have an airborne sex pheromone. While it is unknown if this is true of tarantulas, they do have scented silk. Often, an adult male presented with only silk from the cage of a receptive female will begin courtship. It is a bad sign if you put a male in the cage of a

female and he does nothing but pace. Some males may be so eager to mate that they will court immatures of either sex. Sometimes this mismatched pair will even mate. It may be that the vigorous courtship of an eager male confuses the immature spider. Female tarantulas have their own courtship behavior called a receptivity display. Receptivity displays vary, but may be a wiggle of the first pairs of legs, or a vigorous drum on the substrate with the front feet. If you see this, you can be sure your chances for success are high.

If you have an adult female you intend to breed, there are several things you will want to do in advance of the pairing.

✔ First, make sure the cage is the best you can provide. Females are much more likely to reproduce successfully if they have a retreat. This is not so tricky for arboreal species, but burrowers are harder to accommodate, as I pointed out in the section on housing, beginning on page 20.

Jumping spiders like this one from the family **Salticidae** *are not tarantulas, but they also do not build webs.*

However, it is better to leave a well-adjusted female in a less-sophisticated cage (such as a plastic sweater box) than to move her into a large terrarium and then immediately attempt to mate her. If you do so, you run the risk of having the change of cage stress the spider, which will reduce your chances of a successful mating. Being well fed will put the tarantula in the mood for motherhood, and eventually result in more eggs.

✔ Second, make sure the cage is in a quiet place. Tarantulas are sensitive to the vibrations produced by people moving around the room. The vibration of lots of activity will stress the female and increase the chances she will eat her eggs. Males should also be well fed, but the important thing for them is spinning the sperm web. In the weeks following the final molt, males will spin a hammock-shaped sperm web in the cage (outlined on page 9.) They will also spin a sperm web after mating to recharge their palps.

The Big Night

So here you are—it is early evening, you have an adult pair of conditioned animals, and you (and, we hope, they) are in the mood. When mating tarantulas, always introduce the male to the female's cage. Do not remove them both to a third place; the female must be as calm as possible. I usually place the female's cage on the floor (if it is small), lower the lights, and quietly remove the lid. You may find these preparations melodramatic, but this attention can make the difference between success and failure. I place the cage on the floor so if things go wrong and spiders start running all over, you will not have any of them taking a dive off a tabletop. I then place the male's cage next to the female's, and remove the lid. The male will likely be pacing his cage if he is ready. Try to encourage him to climb into the female's cage by gently prodding him with the cage lid. Also try to arrange it so that he climbs into a part of the female's cage away from the female. This is an important point because you want him to "scent" her before she feels his movements. If he does not have the chance to court the female first, she may grab him for dinner because she has not yet recognized him for what he is. Try not to startle the male either. Startled males blunder into females with disastrous results.

The Courtship Dance

So, you now have a male tarantula in the female's cage. He should begin to slowly pace. When his feet contact the female's silk, he should begin to jiggle slightly. This first shake of his body is the beginning of the courtship dance. The actual display will vary, depending on the species, but will be some combination of full-body jiggles and taps with the front pairs of legs and pedipalps on the ground. He will then start to search the cage for the female. Remember that he is relying on scent at this point (being essentially blind) and may seem to be ignoring the female, but he is actually concentrating on nothing else but finding her. If you have a male that simply walks around the cage, seemingly oblivious, then watch closely for the moment he approaches the female. If he stumbles on her, she may attack. I keep an extralarge pair of forceps handy to keep the pair apart if the female gets aggressive but you can insert anything between a combative pair of tarantulas.

Receptivity

If the female perceives the male's signal and likes what she hears, she should turn to face him. In some species the females will drum on the cage bottom in an unmistakable manner, which is the receptivity display. Once the male has located the female and made physical contact, his tapping will become more frenzied. At this point (unless you and the male are lucky and the female gave a receptivity display), the female is deciding if she wants to mate or eat. It is hard to describe the difference between a female that is receptive and one that is annoyed, as in both cases the female rears up. Angry females will often lash out with their front legs in a striking motion, as they will do when annoyed by a person. If receptive, she will flex at the abdomen-cephalothorax joint more.

The Mating Act

The male will move in and begin to embrace the female from the front. Their legs will intertwine—quite a sight! The male will push the female back and at this point hook his tibial mating spurs under her fangs. Many people have suggested that the male is "restraining" the female with these spurs (even the term "spurs" suggests domination). However, I have never believed this since I saw my first pair of tarantulas mate. I believe that the spurs help the male position the female for mating. I do not think the female could assume that position alone. The female is so much bulkier and stronger than the male that if she did not want to mate, the answer would be "No!" Females seem to enter a trancelike state at this point that must make her seem less threatening to the male. Flexing the body of the female to the degree he does makes it easier

to insert his embolus into her genital aperture. Males mate with both palps alternately. He reaches down past her genital opening, flexes the terminal segment of the palp (bearing the embolus) backward, inserts the tip into the opening, and pulls back toward the female's front end, pulling the palp into the epigastric furrow. The female has two spermathecae and the male inserts his left palp into the left side of her epigastric furrow, even though they are face to face. The male will alternate sides, first one palp, then the other. If both the female and male are absolutely ready, they will mate this way through several rounds of insertions. If the female is wavering in her decision to mate, the male may get only a single (if any!) insertion. If this is the case take the male out immediately and try again in a few weeks.

Once the male is finished, he will start to back off. Watch closely at this point as the female's trance is about to end, and quick! The transition from receptive to annoyed is often so fast it is astounding. The male acts accordingly and the swiftness with which he tries to distance himself from the female is comical. Again, this is where you will be glad to have the cage on the floor. It is worth trying to mate the spiders again in a few weeks. In the meantime, feed the female all she will eat. Wait for the appearance of a new sperm web in the male's cage, which may take a couple of weeks. Do not be anxious if the female is not receptive the second time; this may be a sign she is gravid.

After Mating

Egg production and incubation is the trickiest part. Females of tropical species may lay eggs within weeks after mating; species from

An adult male Mexican blond tarantula (Aphonopelma chalcodes). Note how totally different the male looks from the female.

An adult female redskeleton tarantula (Ephebopus rufescens).

An adult female Mexican redleg tarantula (Brachypelma emilia)

An adult male Trinidad olive tarantula (Hapalopus incei).

A single tarantula egg. This is from a Trinidad chevron tarantula.

A group of Malaysian blackvelvet tarantula postembryos. The eggsac was cut open to view the developing young.

more seasonal areas may take months. With spiders there is no accurately predictable time period between mating and egg laying, and it is not at all comparable to gestation in mammals. Females mature the eggs internally and time to egg laying depends on age, time since the last molt, feeding history, and other factors. The eggs are not fertilized until they are actually being laid. Female tarantulas can store sperm (in the spermatheca), until the next molt. As they shed the lining of their spermatheca when they molt, they lose the sperm and need to mate again to reproduce. So if you have a tarantula that lays eggs and has not been mated since she last shed, she is carrying "duds."

Laying the Eggs

The best you can do at this point is to keep the spider well fed and quiet. If the tarantula was a pet you handled,

stop petting her. If you see her become really fat, rejoice. If she starts to do a lot of digging and spinning silk in the cage, chill the champagne! Terrestrial tarantulas lay eggs by making a bowl-shaped depression in the cage floor

Three tarantula eggsacs: (from left to right) from Malaysian blackvelvet, Bolivian steelyblue, and cobalt blue tarantulas.

(preferably in the retreat). I have not seen what arboreal tarantulas do as they are hidden in their retreats. The bowl-shaped depression determines the size and quality of the egg mass, so being able to dig this bowl is an important step in the process. The female will line this bowl with silk. This may take a while as the silk is quite thick. Then the female deposits the eggs. They are yellow and in a lot of fluid. Most tarantula eggs are approximately the size of peppercorns, or smaller. The female will lay silk over the eggs and then gather the edges of the lining and begin to roll her egg sac. This is a crucial step in egg laying. If the female perceives that the egg sac is misshapen, she may eat the eggs. This is why cage conditions are important. If the female does not have the substrate and space to dig a bowl for egg laying, the prospects for success are poor.

Females will spend quite a lot of time rolling and silking the mass until it is roughly spherical. Then she will settle on it. Most tarantulas carry the eggs in their fangs and otherwise keep in constant physical contact with it. Some African tarantulas are reported to hang their egg sac from the roof of their retreat. If you are foolish enough to try to take the eggs away from any female tarantula, watch out! She will be very aggressive. I would hold off feeding an incubating female, as the prey may disturb her. Try a feeding only after a couple of weeks, and if the female does not immediately eat, take the prey out. Make sure there is water at all times.

Eating the Eggs

Sometimes tarantulas eat their eggs, even after weeks of careful incubation. There are fewer sadder experiences in tarantula keeping than to peek eagerly into the cage of an incubating female and see the egg sac gone. It is not possible with any certainty to say why they eat the eggs but it has been suggested that they can sense if the eggs are infertile. I think it is most likely that disturbance may make them turn cannibal; however, many factors play a role.

Artificial Incubation

The art and science of tarantula egg incubation is still in its infancy. There are almost as many techniques as there are people trying it. I have had limited success with it myself and still prefer letting the female tarantula do it. The most widely used technique is the so-called hammock method. In this case, what you do is suspend the eggs in a fabric hammock in a high-humidity environment. I have used material marketed as bridal veil. This is a very fine mesh made out of a synthetic material. Synthetic stocking material (such as pantyhose) will also work. The important thing is *not* to use a natural fabric such as cheesecloth (made of cotton) since natural fibers will get moldy in a moist environment. Next, take a round, plastic, food-storage box, and cut a large hole into the lid. Put some sand or small stones into the box to stabilize it, and loosely hang a piece of the bridal veiling over the top. Then put the cut-out lid on top to secure the fabric. You now have a weighted, circular hammock for the eggs. Place the hammock inside a larger plastic box with wet paper towels on the bottom, and change the paper toweling often to prevent mold growth. (Don't use free-standing water because the hatching spiderlings will eventually climb out of the hammock and fall into the water and drown.) This larger box should have pin holes put in the lid to admit air but keep out scuttle flies. Don't take the eggs away from the female right away. Apparently the egg sac needs the almost constant massaging that only the female can give them. If you take the eggs away too soon the eggs clump up and won't hatch. After two or three weeks of mom's close attention you can take the eggs way and place them in the hammock. The egg sac should be turned at least once a day. After a week or two more you can cut the egg sac open and lay the eggs directly in the fabric hammock. The advantage of doing this is that you can more closely monitor the development of the eggs and remove the ones that go bad. The disadvantage is that the eggs are now exposed to fungus spores and other infectious agents in the air. Eventually you will see the eggs hatch into the postembryonic stage, which looks like eggs with legs. They will molt again and start to show darkening around the eyes and fangs and some hair. At this stage they may cannibalize any unhatched eggs in the hammock with them. They need to shed again before they are ready to move around on their own and feed like the spiderlings they are. You can take a middle road and leave the egg sac intact. The spiderlings don't need any help to emerge from the silk bag. This may be the best trade-off between the risk of maternal cannibalism and the chance for mold growth leading to losing the entire clutch.

I would suggest that you do not remove eggs from the female's care unless it is a spider with a past history of eating her eggs. Until more is known about what does and does not work with the artificial incubation of spider eggs an element of risk is involved. On the other hand, if we do not try, we will never learn.

The Big Day

One morning after a month (or two or three depending on the species) of nail biting, you will peer into the cage and see a mass of spiderlings. Remember that bottle of champagne? Some tarantulas hatch as hairless postembryos. At this stage they are all but helpless. In several days they will shed into first instar recognizable baby tarantulas. Others go through the first molt in the egg sac. The females of some species, such as pinktoes, are known to feed their young. Baby spiders are all much more tolerant of each other than adults. Only after a period of weeks will you begin to see cannibalism in the nursery. Because of the sheer numbers of babies some people leave the youngsters together at this point to lighten the load of rearing via cannibalism. If this sounds harsh, remember that some species can lay over 1,000 eggs. Surely an embarrassment of riches!

REARING BABIES

So, whether you bought it or bred it, you are the proud owner of a hatchling tarantula. Like most baby animals, very young tarantulas have their charm; however, for the first few molts, they may not resemble their parents very much.

Starting Out

In fact, your new little tarantula may not look like much at all—small, pinkish gray, and not very hairy. Few species are very distinctive when young. Examples of this category are early instar pinktoe tarantulas and goliath pinkfoot tarantulas. Young pinktoe tarantulas are strikingly marked in pale colors and reddish markings; young goliath pinkfoots have pink feet. In both these cases the markings fade with age. But one thing all hatchling tarantulas have in common is an appetite! It is impossible to feed a young tarantula too much. Another common characteristic is their sensitivity to dry conditions; keep them moist whatever the native habitat.

If you bred these baby tarantulas yourself, you are faced with the dilemma of housing and feeding all these spiders. Tarantulas, like most spiders, go through a brief period after hatching when they cluster together on the web, crawling over each other like sociable animals. Only later does their cannibalistic side show itself. During this truce period you can

Getting ready to head out on their own. A group of Mexican redrump tarantula spiderlings shedding.

keep the spiderlings together and even feed them. The length of time they will aggregate peacefully will vary from days to weeks depending on the stage of development of the spiders when they hatched. Some hatch out as small tarantulas, ready to go, while other species hatch out as bald and nearly helpless hatchlings in the postembryo stage and need to go through a molt or two before they feed.

When to Separate the Spiderlings

There are two sure signs that it is time to separate the spiderlings:

1. they start eating each other, and

2. they start attempting to disperse.

Cannibalism will almost always take place. In fact, it has even been found to start inside the egg sac. A symptom of the onset of dispersal behavior is pacing around the cage, looking for an escape. If you feed the aggregated spiderlings in a group, you will benefit those spiderlings ready to eat and delay the day when you have to go through the chore of separating them, but you will also increase the cannibalism rate. The presence of food and the stimulus to hunt will accelerate the expression of the more adult behaviors, including cannibalism. Fortunately, tarantula spiderlings are fairly docile and easy to separate. They will usually just sit there and let you coax them into a vial or jar. If you separate them early, do not worry if they do not immediately fall on their food, as their hunting behaviors may still be suppressed by their young age.

Housing Spiderlings

While adult tarantulas are hardy critters, the youngsters are more delicate. Because of their small body size, they dry out easily; however, if you start with a healthy spiderling and watch the basics, you should have no problems. Hatchling tarantulas are best reared in small containers. You would be doing the little tarantula no favors at all by putting it in a larger cage and waiting for it to grow into it. I have used plastic sandwich boxes, disposable condiment containers (such as the type that holds side dishes in fast food places), pill vials, and baby food jars.

Container Setups

There are two basic kinds of rearing container setups: those for arboreal species, and those for terrestrial species. In the container for the terrestrial species you need only some kind of substrate kept moist. For arboreal species use a taller container and add a piece of stick or bark for the little spider to attach a silk retreat. While terrestrial tarantula spiderlings are not likely to attempt to dig a burrow right away, arboreals will usually spin a retreat right from the start. This is to be encouraged as they will be less water-stressed and molt with fewer problems in a retreat.

Bedding

Any of the beddings recommended in the section on substrates (see page 22) will work. I use peat moss; many use vermiculite. *Never* use sand or gravel. Even though sand and gravel are fine for adult tarantulas native to dry desert regions, all spiderlings need to be treated as the most delicate native of moist tropical regions. If you keep the sand moist, mold growth is much higher than for the suggested alternatives. If you are rearing the spiderling in a container too small for a water dish, it is not a problem if the substrate is kept moist at all times. This statement may seem at first to fly in the face of all I have said about the importance of water; however, all small spiders can drink what is called capillary water, which is the water absorbed into the substrate. Because you will be keeping your little spider at a higher humidity by keeping the substrate wetter than you would when it gets older, the substrate will be wet enough to drink from. For arboreal spiders spray the webbing regularly. Do not *ever* let the cage of a small tarantula spiderling dry out, or it will die.

Setting Up the Housing

To set up the housing simply take the container you choose, put a half inch (13 mm) or so of the moistened substrate at the bottom, and put the spider in. The ventilation holes on the lid should be small and few. Don't use wire mesh as this will lead to too much air movement and evaporation. Tarantula respiration takes place at a very low rate, so suffocation is not a problem even with minimal ventilation, but water loss is a big problem. Only immature-to-adult tarantulas can keep their water balance by drinking and not dry out.

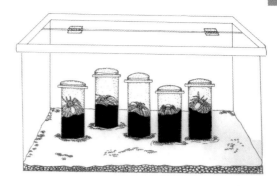

Very young tarantulas in individual vials in a humidified case. Proper attention to humidity is crucial to successfully rearing very young tarantulas because of their small size. They can quickly dry out and die of dehydration or have molting problems.

Feeding

As I mentioned above, you cannot feed a tarantula spiderling too much; they will eat far more often than they will when adult. A hatchling tarantula is busy growing and has an appetite that is hard to satisfy. Unlike adult spiders, very young tarantulas pause in their eating only to molt. Even then, the molt cycle is much faster in younger spiders. They may go from premolt lethargy to the shed and back to ravenous in less than a week when very young. The same process may last well over a month in an older spider. Hatchling tarantulas can starve to death in weeks, even though adults can live years with no food. I have noticed that spiderlings that are not fed soon after they disperse from the mother's web have a much higher mortality rate than spiderlings fed well immediately. None of this is in your control if you buy your spiderling from a breeder after a molt or two. If it looks fat and happy, it probably is. Be aware that the spiderlings of some of the more slow-growing species may go off-feed for longer periods before the molt than others.

If you are confronted with a hatch of hundreds of hatchling tarantulas, you are best off separating them as soon as you can and feeding them immediately. Starved hatchlings have a slower initial growth rate when fed and higher mortality rate. My advice is to feed them early and often and give away any you cannot rear or sell. Even with the best of care you will notice that in any group of spiderlings there are some that thrive and others that never seem to do really well. How much this is due to genetic differences or if those that do particularly well got a head start by eating their siblings is unknown.

If you have only one or a few spiderlings, you can dote on them and feed them as often as they will eat. In any case, feed them at least twice a week. You can also increase growth rate by rearing them at warmer temperatures, such as mid to upper 80s°F (30s°C). The need for food will slow with age. If you restrict their food when young, they will also not grow as large when they mature. Also, the quality of diet is more important for younger than older spiders. Diversity is the key to success. Very small spiders are hard to feed as it is very hard to find a reliable source for small food items. Thus, you may have to raise your own. At first you can feed them vestigial-winged fruit flies, then flour beetle larvae, small mealworms, and small crickets. A discussion of food follows in the next chapter.

CATCHING FOOD AND CARING FOR YOUR SICK TARANTULA

There are a variety of options for feeding your hungry arachnids. Again, it's important to realize that a diverse diet is a balanced diet.

What's for Dinner?

If you are feeding only one to a half-dozen specimens, then you can rely on store-bought foods, such as crickets and mealworms. You can also catch foods in the wild if you are lucky enough to live in a place where there are natural areas. One thing I advise is to resist the temptation to offer potentially dangerous prey to the tarantula's cage in order to watch a fight. Feeding larger beetles and grasshoppers, wasps, or even other arachnids can result in injury to your spider. A good rule of thumb is that the body length of the food item should be half the body length (or less) of the tarantula. (Obvious exceptions to this rule are earthworms and beetle larvae.) Food items should also be something you can hold in your hand without fear of getting bitten or stung.

A skeleton tarantula eating a katydid.

Finding Commercial Sources

Most pet shops stock crickets and mealworms, which are fine for feeding older juvenile or adult tarantulas as a basic diet. Some stores that trade heavily in reptiles may offer wax moth larvae as well. Other potential feeder bugs for tarantulas are nightcrawlers that pet shops sometimes carry for feeding large fish such as cichlids. You will be lucky indeed to find a pet store stocking fruit flies or very small crickets. If you have a large and aggressive tarantula, you can even feed it small mice and goldfish. Bait shops are a good source for cheap feeder bugs. Remember, the commercial worm- and insect-rearing business got its start supplying the recreational fishing trade, not people feeding tarantulas! The bulk of the business for these people is still for fishing bait. I have found crickets, wax moth larvae, mealworms, and, of course, earthworms at bait shops.

There are commercial sources for other types of feeder insects. Biological supply catalogs offer many kinds of insects for lab rearing. The aquarium and reptile hobby magazines (see Information, page 109) also run ads for individuals dealing in harder to find food insects such as vestigial-winged fruit flies and house flies; however, unless you have a large collection you should not have to branch out too radically from a few basic insects for food.

Domestic Gray Crickets (Acheta domestica)

Domestic crickets are native to Eurasia and are a pest there. Crickets are related to cockroaches and share many of their traits. They eat anything, they are hardy, and they breed constantly. Crickets have not only been cultivated in captivity but domesticated in the sense that they have been selectively bred to enhance their growth rate and fecundity under commercial rearing conditions. Crickets are the basic diet for any tarantula-rearing operation as they are relatively easy to keep and rear and they are among the more nutritious food insects. I have reared tarantulas to a fertile adulthood on crickets alone, although I do not recommend it. There are many commercial cricket farms across the country now supplying crickets of all sizes year-round. No hatchling tarantula is too small to eat a hatchling cricket. Unless you have a lot of tarantulas or are feeding reptiles too, you will not want to order crickets directly from the supplier as they are sold in lots of 500 or 1,000.

Keeping crickets: Crickets need dry, warm conditions to do well. They like to sit near a heat source such as a light bulb. They are flightless and cannot climb up a smooth sur-

face. (They can jump, of course.) Crickets are easily kept in a 10-gallon (38-L) aquarium. You will want to put on a lid if you are keeping adult crickets. A strip of smooth-surfaced wide tape (such as strapping tape) around the inside top will keep the crickets from climbing out. A 2- to 3-inch (5–7 cm) band of petroleum jelly smeared around the top will also do the job. The tank does not need any kind of bedding. In fact, a barren tank is far easier to clean. Put in cardboard egg carton material or the cardboard rolls from paper towels and toilet paper for the crickets to climb on. Food can be just about anything. Commercial cricket farmers recommend chicken feed, but you can use dry dog food, breakfast cereal, raw potatoes, apples, carrots, or lettuce. Water should be supplied in a glass vial with a plug of cotton in the end lying on its side. If you put the water in a dish, put in gravel or a sponge so the crickets do not drown. I recommend feeding a good-quality dry dog food supplemented with raw fruits and vegetables. Adult crickets live about two weeks so you cannot stockpile them. When handling them for feeding, use your hand or tweezers. If you need to feed a lot of crickets you may find it worthwhile to chill them in the refrigerator for 15 to 20 minutes to slow them down. This cuts down on crickets escaping.

Fruit Flies (Drosophila melanogaster)

A culture of vestigial-winged fruit flies is very handy for starting hatchling tarantulas. Unfortunately, fruit flies are deficient in amino acids (such as linoleic acid) so they are not suitable to feed as more than half the diet of a growing tarantula. You can add linoleic acid to the fly culture medium, which helps, but the usefulness of fruit flies is unfortunately limited. Spiders fed too long on fruit flies alone develop molting problems and curly legs, which is too bad as fruit flies are so easy to raise once you have the rearing medium. You can catch wild fruit flies in most places, but the wild winged variety is of limited use for tarantula food unless the spiderlings are in very small containers and can encounter the flies. There are two routes to go with the fruit flies: buying from a reptile food dealer, or spending the money to buy a starter culture of the vestigial-winged strain of flies and rearing medium mix from a biological supply house.

Keeping and breeding fruit flies: The folks selling flies through the mail send a well-started culture bottle that will produce flies for weeks. If you buy flies this way, you will be out of flies when the rearing medium dries up. The commercial rearing medium sold by biological supply houses comes as dry flakes. Mix these dry flakes with water (1:1 by volume), sprinkle a pinch of yeast on top, and add flies. After about two weeks you will have hundreds of flies. You could try rearing the vestigial-winged flies on fruit, but wild fruit flies would come in (as they inevitably will), mate with the vestigial-winged flies, and soon all your flies will have full wings. Buying the culture medium and flies from a biological supply house is less expensive in the long run. I mix the rearing medium up in 16-ounce (500 mL) juice bottles to a depth of about an inch and a half (4 cm) and stopper the bottles with a piece of foam or cotton. The flies are easier to handle if you first stun them with cold. I do this by shaking the

Domestic crickets are easily housed. All they really need is food, water, and a place to climb.

flies out of the culture bottle into a plastic vial and putting the vial in the refrigerator until they are lying on the bottom, perhaps 20 minutes. If you chill the whole culture bottle, many of the flies will get stuck to the medium.

Mealworms (Tenebrio molitor)

There was a time, not long ago, when the humble mealworm was all we had to feed captive spiders and reptiles from the pet shop. Mealworms are actually the larvae of a beetle. But, before you imagine them as "slimy creepy crawlies," let me tell you that these larvae have a hard, dry cuticle and therefore are not slimy like earthworms. Mealworms are pests of stored grain. Being pests, mealworms are ridiculously easy to rear, can be stored in the refrigerator, and are easy to buy. The only drawback is that they are not very active and therefore not as attractive to spiders for food. They have a way of slowly crawling out of sight (or should I say touch) of the spider. They are a fine food source and can be reared so that you have access to a variety of sizes, which is so important to feeding those spiderlings.

Keeping and rearing mealworms: To rear mealworms buy several plastic shoe boxes and

fill each two-thirds full of a mix of grain products. Oatmeal, corn meal, or bran flakes are all readily available in the grocery store. For moisture, put a piece of carrot or raw potato on top, add mealworms, and stand back. Make sure the box is well ventilated to keep the moisture levels down. Excess moisture will lead to mold growth, and mold growth on the cereal will kill the mealworms. I suggest staggering the start date for the cultures so you do not wind up with all beetles in a few weeks. After a few weeks you will see shiny black beetles about an inch long (2.54 cm) running around on top of the cereal. Even if you do not want to rear mealworms they will be better food for the spiders after fattening up. The ones you buy in the pet shop in a little plastic cup are usually a bit dried out and thin from sitting around in the refrigerator. Also, the activity level of the worms are increased if they are recently fed, making them a more attractive food for the spiders.

Flour Beetles (Tribolium sp.)

Other pests of stored grain are flour beetles. These are related to mealworms but are much smaller and even easier to rear. Flour beetles are about one-fifth the size of mealworm beetles. I like to use flour beetle larvae to feed very young tarantulas because of their size. You can also buy flour beetles from biological supply houses; there are two species used in studies of population genetics, *T. confusum* and *T. castaneum*. However, as they are pests, you can find them in bags of flour that have been stored too long.

Keeping and rearing flour beetles: As I said above, flour beetles are even easier to rear than mealworms because they do not need a moisture source; flour is enough. Use whole-wheat flour mixed with white flour in a one-to-one ratio. Because the larvae are so small, the best way to use them as food is to sift them out of the flour with a wire strainer, then pick them out of the strained material (concentrated beetles, pupae, and shed skins) with a tweezers. I do not use the adults, only the larvae. One drawback to flour beetles as food is that the larvae are hairy, which means that the flour will adhere to them. This flour will eventually grow mold in the tarantula-rearing container. I solved this by bouncing the worms off the tabletop to get rid of the flour before feeding them to the spiders. You only need to drop them several inches to do the trick.

Superworms (Zophobas sp.)

The third beetle in the family Tenebrionidae is a recent arrival on the food bug scene—the tropical "superworm." Superworms, as the name suggests, have the advantage of large size. They are found in decayed wood in the wild but have been domesticated for feeding reptiles and are an excellent food source for larger spiders. They are not usually stocked by pet stores but can be found for sale in the reptile-keeping magazines. Because they are not pests of stored grain they are a little trickier to culture than their poor cousins the mealworms and flour beetles.

Keeping superworms: Superworms cannot be refrigerated because they are tropical. This means that you have to either use up any superworms you buy shortly after buying them or keep them fed and healthy. Superworm larvae in nature feed on decayed wood but can be kept in captivity on sawdust or peat moss. Moisture can be supplied by offering vegetables such as carrots or potatoes (as for mealworms).

False Death's Head Cockroach (Blaberus discoidales)

Perhaps the very best cockroach to breed for tarantula food is the false death's head cockroach. The adults are a handsome reddish gold color, and the nymphs are attractively marked in light brown with light spots. They are native to the New World tropics. These are leaf-litter cockroaches that cannot climb smooth surfaces such as glass. This is an obvious advantage for keeping them. In this species, the adults do get wings and can fly under some circumstances, but I have not had any escapes.

Keeping and Rearing False Death's Head Cockaroaches

I breed these in a 10- or 20-gallon (40- or 80-L) aquarium with a layer of dry pine shavings on the bottom. I also put a band of plastic strapping tape around the inside so the cockroaches cannot climb out the corners of the tank. They will eat about anything but they particularly seem to relish lettuce, oranges, and bananas.

Other Food Bugs

Wax moth larvae and cockroaches are good food sources for tarantulas. Wax moth larvae are the caterpillars of yet another pest species, the greater wax moth (*Galleria mellonella*). This moth is a pest in bee-keeping operations where it eats bees' wax. The larvae are not relying on the wax alone for nutrition, but the remains of bee larvae in the comb. Rearing moths is more specialized so I recommend buying them. They are plump, soft larvae about 1 inch (2.5 cm) in length. They are a good supplement to a tarantula's diet and can be purchased at some pet shops, bait shops, and from hobby magazines. Unfortunately, they do not store well and are sold in cups of wood shavings just before pupating. If you buy any you will need to use them up in a week or two as they will soon pupate at room temperature and they do not survive refrigeration well.

Earthworms are a good food source for the larger spider. I have used nightcrawlers (*Lumbricus* sp.) as a staple diet for large goliath birdeater tarantulas that ignored crickets. Nightcrawlers are sold in small lots at bait shops and some pet shops and can be stored in the refrigerator.

Tarantulas are certainly less prone to sickness than tropical fish, reptiles, or amphibians, for example. This is just as well, as virtually no veterinarian would know what to do if presented with a sick spider. You might be lucky enough to find an individual willing to experiment (all those dogs and cats do get a bit boring!) but most will be unable or even unwilling to help treat an arachnid. So, you need to be willing to try for yourself. I offer the following suggestions as guidelines for possible treatments. I am not a veterinarian, and the following information is based only on my own experiences with tarantulas and other arachnids and the experiences of colleagues.

Traumatized Tarantulas

As I mentioned in the section on handling (see page 38), you need to guard against falls. The prognosis for recovery for any tarantula that has had a fall severe enough to cause bleeding from the pedicel or abdomen is poor. However, the most important thing to do for any spider that suffers loss of body fluid is to get it a drink of water. As I mentioned in the first chapter, spiders have a partially hydraulic muscle system and extend their legs using blood pressure, not muscles. Therefore, if they lose blood (more properly called hemolymph), they need to drink to replace the blood fluid volume lost.

Puncture Wounds

Occasionally a tarantula will receive a puncture in the abdomen, a much more serious wound than any to a leg. If a tarantula suffers a puncture wound, it can be plugged with an adhesion patch. You will have to consider how to hold the spider so you can patch the wound. One possibility is to use the restrained handling procedures described on page 38. The shortcoming of this technique is that the spider will drive up its blood pressure when it struggles and thus hasten blood loss. Another solution is to anesthetize the spider by chilling it in the refrigerator for 15–20 minutes. For a bandage, I have used a small piece of plastic with petroleum jelly on it slapped over the leak. If the spider can reach the bandage, it will pull it off, so you may need to try a blob of petroleum jelly alone. An alternative is to use a fast-drying adhesive (such as Superglue). The wounded area will be completely healed at the next molt, although you may notice a slight discoloration.

Leg Loss

If a tarantula loses a leg it is in far better shape than you might imagine, as most can grow another one. Spiders have the ability to shed legs the way some lizards shed tails. Better to lose a leg than your life, especially if you have eight to begin with! All spiders have a specialized joint in their legs near the base (between the coxa and trochanter), which breaks away when the leg is grabbed. The open stump is closed off by muscular contraction at the joint and blood loss is immediately stopped. This process is called autotomy (or autospasy by some authors) and is an important way for the injured tarantula to save blood. In fact, if a leg is injured in any way the tarantula may decide that it is more trouble than it is worth and pull it off itself. Rather bizarrely, tarantulas will often eat the leg so as not to lose the nutrients they invested in growing it in the first place.

The leg will not be totally replaced in one molt. How well developed the leg is after the first posttrauma shed will depend on how long before the actual molt the leg was lost. If they lose the leg just before a molt, they may not have time to grow a new leg under the old cuticle. It is certainly amaz-

YOUR SICK TARANTULA

ing to see the size of the old leg stump and then the size of the leg that appears after the molt, small though it is. In any case, it will take several sheds for the regenerated leg to match its mate on the other side of the spider. Insults to the cuticle can also speed up the timing of the next molt, which is the spider's way of healing itself.

Having a Bad Molt

Shedding is a big event for a tarantula, and things can go wrong. For the geriatric tarantula the best thing you can do is offer water. In many cases the bleeding will clot on its own. All tarantulas, particularly young ones, can fail to shed old skin if they are kept too dry. For tarantulas that get stuck in the old skin, water is again the main therapeutic agent. This can be as minor as having a patch of old cuticle stick to the abdomen. In this case you can soften the dry skin with water and gently pull the old skin off. Do not just jerk the old skin off, but gently pull at it (with the spider trying to go in the other direction by now), and if it peels away, success is yours. Occasionally, tarantulas fail to free old legs. This can be a real crisis depending on how many legs are stuck and how deep it is. If the legs are most of the way out and stuck, then you might be able to soften the old skin with water and gently pull the old skin off. If the legs are stuck most of the way in, forced autotomy may be your best choice. If only one or two legs are stuck, you can induce autotomy of the stuck legs by pinching them through the old cuticle using a tweezers. If most (or sometimes all) legs get stuck and the new cuticle has already hardened, I am sorry to say your best bet in this case is to euthanize the spider. I do this by placing the poor creature in the freezer.

Cuticular Conditions

Fungal infections: Rarely you will notice a gray patch on the abdomen of a tarantula. This

Petroleum jelly can be used to plug small puncture wounds on a tarantula. Only use it for areas of the body the tarantula cannot reach with its feet as you see here. Also, keep it away from the openings of the book lungs or the spider may suffocate.

discoloration will not come off with a spray from a water bottle like dirt and is probably a fungal infection. Fungal infections most often occur in moister caging situations. I do not know if the fungus is attacking something on the cuticle of the spider or if it can go deeper. One of the first things to do is let the cage dry out. This will slow or stop the growth of the fungus. You can try treating the fungus with a topical treatment, but this should be considered experimental. When the spider molts, the fungus will be shed with the old cuticle and you should not see it again.

Lumps: I have had adult female tarantulas develop lumps on the abdomen for no apparent reason. This seemed to be correlated with advanced age in the spider. I have had tarantulas molt out of these, leaving a discolored area on the new cuticle. Tarantulas can develop bleeding from the joints after a molt, particularly when older. I suspect that these lumps are areas where blood has leaked in between the layers of cuticle, which is in keeping with the leaky cuticle condition I mentioned earlier. Lumps on the abdomen are more serious, but remain enigmatic at this time.

OTHER ARACHNIDS

If you like tarantulas, you are likely to find other arachnids interesting. There are smaller spider species that are often locally available, easy to maintain, and fun to watch.

Other types of arachnids make an intriguing comparison to spiders and are fairly easy to maintain in captivity. These are scorpions, whipscorpions (or vinegaroons), tailless whip-scorpions, and windscorpions (also called sun spiders, solfugids, or camel spiders).

Other Spiders

There are several types of spiders sometimes offered for sale, or encountered in the wild, that you may want to keep. This includes the nontheraphosid mygalomorphs (trapdoor spiders and allies) and the "true" or araneomorph spiders (widows, large orbweavers, and various hunting spiders). I categorize the araneomorph spiders here for convenience as web-building spiders and non-web-building, or hunting, spiders.

Trapdoor Spiders and Relatives

Tarantulas are closely related to several spider families that are more widespread in distribution than tarantulas. These tarantula relatives occur as far north as New York State in the United States and Britain in Europe.

An adult female red widow (**Latrodectus bishopi**).

They are the trapdoor spiders (the family Ctenizidae), the purseweb spiders (the family Atypidae), and the foldingdoor spiders (the family Antrodiaetidae). Some arachnological sources refer to all mygalomorphs as tarantulas, but this is a term I reserve for the Theraphosidae alone.

All mygalomorphs are an arachnological novelty as they share many primitive features with the hypothesized ancestral spider (see Understanding Tarantulas, beginning on page 5). They make an interesting contrast to tarantulas as they are even more adapted to life in a burrow. They have shorter legs, are not as agile on the ground as a theraphosid, and are almost totally hairless. Trapdoor spiders are sometimes offered for sale by dealers. If you live in the eastern United States or in Europe, these nontheraphosid mygalomorphs are the closest you will get to seeing tarantulas in the wild without making a major trip. Unfortunately, most non-theraphosid mygalomorphs are obligate burrowers to an even greater extent than any tarantula. As a result, keeping them without the opportunity to burrow would be stressful to the spiders and shorten their lives. This means that you will have to house them in a soil-filled cage and allow them to burrow, and, as a result, you will almost never see them.

Hunting wild mygalomorphs takes an element of luck or exact location data. All these spiders do an excellent job of camouflaging their retreats and finding them is not easy even if you have information on a locale.

The trapdoor spiders and foldingdoor spiders are found in their highest densities on road banks or stream banks. The trapdoor is an amazing bit of spider engineering. The spiders make a perfectly fitting door of silk and soil, which they attach to the burrow mouth with a silk hinge.

The folding door of foldingdoor spiders is a collar of silk that the spider can pull shut. Foldingdoor spider burrows are easier to spot than the cunningly constructed trapdoor of the trapdoor spider. I have seen foldingdoor spider burrows in high densities along a road bank in east Tennessee and once found a colony in a small city park in the middle of Cincinnati, Ohio.

Purseweb spiders build a silk tube up the side of a tree and rarely emerge at all. These tubes are camouflaged with dirt and debris. The spiders wait inside and feed by pulling insects through the silk.

You are likely to be made aware of these spiders in your area by the arrival of wandering males in the late summer and fall. There is no mistaking adult male mygalomorphs for anything else. Their size, shiny color, bulky body, and short legs are all diagnostic. Purseweb spider males wander during the day looking for the females' retreats. Because the female purseweb spiders build their retreats on the sides of trees, these males may be using vision to locate the tree trunks. Some of these spider males are brightly marked in black and red and it has been suggested that they may

be mimicking ants to avoid predation by visual, day-active predators such as birds. As always, a brief consideration of what little is known about the mygalomorph spiders yields more questions than answers.

Keeping trapdoor spiders and relatives: If you buy or collect mygalomorph spiders, I recommend a tank setup as for the obligate burrowing tarantulas. Let the spider build its own burrow. If you are lucky enough to have collected the spider yourself, you can attempt to imitate the natural habitat. However, once the burrow is established, you may never see your spider again. Any food you put in will disappear and that will be the only evidence that there is a spider living in the cage. You may be able to induce the spider to build next to the glass, which would allow observation.

Widow Spiders

The widow spiders are a worldwide genus that includes several species of widow spider in North America (*Latrodectus* spp.). The good news about widow spiders is that they are beautiful and hardy; the bad news is that their venom is dangerous to humans. I emphatically do *not* recommend any of the widow spiders to anyone because of this. What is worse than the risk of the bite of an adult kept in captivity is that the spiderlings are minuscule and so can readily escape from a container. If you feel you *must* have a widow spider, please do your family and neighbors a favor—remove any egg sacs the spider lays and take them to a natural area far from human habitation or pop them into the freezer. The females grow much larger than the males. In fact, male black widows have very different markings from the adult female (as do the small immatures).

The Widows of North America

Black widows are undeniably beautiful. The shiny black and red markings of an adult female black widow spider are a sight to behold. There are five species of widow spider in the United States: *L. mactans*, the southern black widow; *L. variolus*, the northern black widow; *L. hesperus*, the western black widow; *L. geometricus*, the brown widow; and *L. bishopi*, the red widow. The first three, *L. mactans*, *L. hesperus*, and *L. variolus*, are typical black widows. The adult females are shiny black with red markings on the abdomen. The famous hourglass marking on the ventral side of the abdomen is best developed in the southern and western widows and may be divided into two red marks in the northern species. Black widows are typically found in dry, sandy, or rocky areas. In the western United States this includes a lot more territory than in the East. In the western states widows can become amazingly common around human habitation. They like our sheds and woodpiles for web building and also like to eat the insects we attract. In the northern parts of their range widow spiders are spotty in distribution. They occur as far north as Canada at sunny, rocky sites, not because they like hot, dry conditions, but rather, they are sensitive to cold. Exposed, sunny sites stay warmer in the winter months.

Brown widow spiders have traveled with humans to the warmer regions of the world. They are thought to be native to Africa. They are humbly marked in browns with a red hourglass and are not as strikingly marked as black widows. If fact, they may be readily mistaken for a common house spider (*Achaearanea tepidariorum*) if not examined carefully. One of the most distinctive traits of the brown widow spiders is their egg sac. Most spiders in the family that contain the widows (the Theridiidae, which also includes many common, inconspicuous, and harmless species) lay spherical, pale brown egg sacs in their web. The brown widow's egg sac has all these features, plus conspicuous tufts all over the surface; there is no mistaking it. If you go brown widow spider hunting, pay attention to any egg sacs you find hanging in tangled webs. They have become established in Florida and build their webs in and around buildings and junk.

Red widows are the most beautiful and rare of the American widow spiders. They have red legs and cephalothorax, and a gray abdomen marked with red. You are not likely to come across red widows as they are found only in the dry, sandy upland habitats of Florida (called "scrub") and are potentially threatened because scrub habitats are threatened. They build their tangled web in the fronds of palmettos well off the ground.

Keeping widows in captivity: Widow spiders are extremely easy to maintain in captivity. They will readily build their tangled web in any container you put them in. A generous container would be some kind of plastic jar or box at least half a gallon (2 L) in volume with an array of sticks for web attachment. You can put in any substrate you like, although this is not necessary. Ventilation can be provided by several holes in the top. You will want to keep the container dry and supply water by misting the web once every week or two. Unlike tarantulas, widows need dryer conditions.

Fortunately for the keeper, female widows are clumsy off their web. If you need to transfer a widow to another cage it is fairly easy to do. You can either reach into the container with a

Now you see it, and now you don't!
The well-camouflaged burrow entrance
of a Trindadian trapdoor spider.

stick, wind up the webbing, and transfer the silk-covered stick with the spider hanging on to the other container, or dump the now webless spider into the new container. Obviously, do not let the spider walk on your unprotected hand! Also, be careful when you remove egg sacs as the female can be very defensive.

Widow spiders will eat just about any insect. And they can take quite large insects, thanks to their web. Once the adult female widow spider is fat, she will be able to survive many months without food. If you have a female widow laying egg sacs, she can lay many of them in sequence. Ideally, you will have acquired an immature female and she will remain infertile (though she may still lay eggs). Unmated widows do not present the hazard of infestation that a fertile female would.

Giant Orbweavers

There are several families of spiders that spin orb webs, the typical wheel-shaped spider web we think of when we say "spider." Two of these orbweaver families have spectacular genera. The first is the genus *Argiope*, in the family Araneidae, and the second is *Nephila*, in the family Tetragnathidae. Spiders in the genus *Argiope* (pronounced "r-guy-o-pee") are called argiope orbweavers and the *Nephila* are referred to as golden silk orbweavers. Both these genera are worldwide in distribution, with golden silk orbweavers being restricted to warmer latitudes than argiope orbweavers.

The argiope orbweaver is one of the largest and most conspicuous spiders in North America. There are several species found in the United States, with two being common: *A. aurantia* and *A. trifasciata*. In Europe there is *A. bruennichi*. Wherever found, argiope orbweavers are inhabitants of open grassy areas. All are marked in metallic colors (that reflect heat) and yellow bands. All have the habit of spinning white silk banners (called stabilimenta) in their webs, that are thought to warn birds from flying into their webs, which would destroy them. Because the argiope orbweavers are so big and strikingly marked, they are readily noticed and, even if you don't want to keep any, once your friends know you are "into" spiders they will want to tell you about seeing these. The northern forms of argiope orbweaver are highly seasonal, with the big,

A large fishing spider (Dolomedes tenebrosus), *common in the eastern U.S.*

A common huntsman spider (Heteropoda venatoria). *This spider is found around the world in tropical and subtropical regions in human habitations.*

conspicuous females being seen in late summer. Dealers sometimes carry the tropical species *A. argentata*, the silver argiope, which is easier to breed in captivity. The silver argiope orbweaver is also found in Florida and Texas in the United States.

The golden silk orbweaving spiders are unusual in that they spin yellow webs. There is no clear reason for this. It has been suggested that they are getting rid of metabolic wastes in their silk. The golden orbweavers are found in warmer climates; in the New World, *N. clavipes* is found from coastal South Carolina to Brazil. In the Old World, there are two species occasionally seen for sale: *N. madagascariensis* from East Africa and the islands of the Indian Ocean, and *N. maculata* from Asia. These last two species are quite large, being the biggest orbweaving spiders. In nature the golden silk orbweaving spiders can be found building their webs in groups in areas with abundant food.

Keeping orbweaving spiders: Both orbweavers are fairly easy to keep in captivity. Any large, airy screen cage will do the trick. A cage can range in size from about 2 feet (60 cm) cubed for argiope orbweaving spiders

to 1 yard (1 m) cubed for golden silk orbweaving spiders. You can also use a design called a window cage. Window cages are generally two panes of glass or pieces of sheet plastic held approximately 6 inches (15 cm) apart by a frame with wire mesh on it. These are sometimes offered for sale by biological supply houses, but they are expensive. The important feature for any orbweaver cage is air movement, so any cage should be at least partially made of wire mesh. It is also possible to release these spiders into a porch or sunny window well and have them build their web there. Feed these spiders by placing crickets in the web. If the cricket will not stick to the web, you can sometimes gently hand-feed the spider by brushing the cricket against the spider's mouth parts. It may help to crush the cricket's head. Water is supplied by misting the webs daily.

Tropical species of both the golden silk orbweaver and the argiope orbweaver can be bred in large colony cages. The species from more seasonal latitudes can be bred too, but the eggs may hatch only if subjected to temperature and humidity fluctuations that match their native environments. These colony cages need to be very big, at least a yard and a half (150 cm) cubed, and well supplied with food such as house flies.

While argiope orbweavers and golden silk orbweaving spiders are fairly easy to please, other types of web spiders can be hard (or impossible) to induce to build webs in captivity. If you collect a web spider yourself, be warned that it may not cooperate. If the spider does not build a web, it will not eat. If you get a spider that will not build a web, you can try a larger cage. If you caught the spider yourself, release it and try another one.

Hunting Spiders

There are many interesting spiders that do not build webs and are not tarantulas. Jumping spiders (family Salticidae), the nursery web spiders (family Pisauridae), and wolf spiders (family Lycosidae) are worldwide and are common. All these can be captured locally, housed simply, and released when the keeper's interest wanes. Housing should mimic the natural habitat of the spider. Usually a simple plastic box with some substrate and a small water dish will do the trick.

I am only going to treat two families of spiders at greater length: the giant crab spiders (family Heteropodidae) and wandering spiders (family Ctenidae). These spiders are noteworthy as they are large, hairy, found in the tropics, and sometimes offered for sale by dealers. They are frequently confused with tarantulas. However, these spiders are *fast!* They are cursorial hunters (meaning running) of cockroaches and are often found in human habitations in warmer regions, including Florida. Both have

very long legs that are held flattened against the substrate and bent forward at the patella joint when the spider is sitting still. This posture is most notable in the giant crab spider, and gives them their distinctive crablike posture.

Heteropoda venatoria is the species most commonly offered for sale. This spider has been very successful in following humans around the warmer parts of the world, living in houses and eating cockroaches. Both giant crab spiders and wandering spiders hide during the day and come out at night to sit by their retreat and wait for dinner. Trying to catch them is quite an exercise because of their speed and agility. These spiders can give a nasty bite, and are very aggressive, so watch out. There is a ctenid in the New World tropics (*Phoneutria ferox*) that is very poisonous and potentially fatal to humans. Female giant crab spiders carry their disk-shaped egg sac under their body.

Keeping giant crab spiders and wandering spiders: These spiders are easy to keep. They are best housed the same way as arboreal tarantulas. They need a spacious cage with pieces of bark to climb on. A 10-gallon (40 L) aquarium tank standing on end would be fine. Substrate such as bark chips can be added as a source for humidity, although this is optional. The main thing to keep in mind is the speed and agility of these spiders; they are great escape artists. They will feed ravenously on crickets and other insects.

Scorpions

Scorpions are easily as famous (or infamous) as tarantulas. Scorpions are among the most ancient lineages of all terrestrial life; the first animal to leave the primordial seas is thought to have been a scorpion. Scorpions are in the order Scorpiones, having a taxonomic rank equivalent to the spiders (order Araneae), in the class Arachnida. If you are interested in tarantulas, you have likely considered acquiring a scorpion as well. There are several species that are easy and interesting to keep and I will treat these here; however, there are many that are so dangerous and uninteresting looking that anyone seeking to buy one has to be doing it for all the wrong reasons. Many of the more striking looking scorpions are *less dangerous* to keep. It is often the small, nondescript ones that can kill you. If someone offers you one of the small, yellow or straw-colored scorpions from the Middle East or North Africa, resist the temptation. There is no sensible reason at all for a beginner to keep one of the more dangerous species when the alternatives are so attractive. One of the large, shiny, black scorpions from tropical Africa or Asia makes a fine pet, and is not likely to kill you. This seems like a simple choice to me! The most dangerous scorpions are in the genera *Androctonus* (from the Old World) and *Centruroides* and *Tityus* (in the New World). *Centruroides* is found in the United States.

All scorpions spend most of their time in burrows or under rocks and fallen logs. They will come out at night only to forage, like tarantulas. Some live in association with a burrow they construct and stay with it for life. Scorpions can live for years. They are generally restricted to the warmer parts of the globe, but do range up into southern Ohio in the United States and the Alps in Europe. Scorpions fluoresce under ultraviolet light. The glow is an eerie green or blue under a black light. There is no clear function for this phenomenon, which is a by-product of the molecular structure of the cuticle. This odd feature of scorpions has been exploited by researchers and collectors who use a handheld black light to find scorpions in the field.

Scorpions have live birth and the young scorpions climb up onto the female's back and ride around until their first molt. Newborn scorpions (called nymphs) are soft and white, and look very helpless. Female scorpions feed their young. Some genera of scorpions are somewhat social (such as *Heterometrus* and *Pandinus*) and the youngsters need to be fed by the mother or they will starve. Male scorpions look just like females except that in many genera they tend to be smaller and have longer, more slender tails (more properly called the postabdomen). If you can look over a group, you can usually spot the difference. Scorpions mate by passing a package of sperm (called a spermatophore). The males and females engage in an elaborate courtship dance, pincers clasped. The males deposit the spermatophore on the ground and guide the female over it so she can pick it up in her genital aperture.

Keeping scorpions: Scorpions are easy to keep. They will do well in any container with substrate, a piece of bark to hide under, and a water dish. How sandy the substrate is and how moist you keep the cage will depend on whether it is a desert or rain forest species. I will treat only four genera here: the Asian forest scorpions (*Heterometrus spinifer* and *H. longimanus*), the African emperor scorpions (*Pandinus imperator, P. dictator*, and *P. gambiensis*), the Arizona hairy scorpion (*Hadrurus arizonensis*), and the South African rock scorpion (*Hadogenes troglodytes*).

A hairy scorpion (**Hadrurus** *sp.*) *seen under normal lighting.*

Asian Forest Scorpions and African Emperor Scorpions

These scorpions are the big, blue-black scorpions that make the best captives. Most of the scorpions currently available commercially are the African emperor scorpions. This may change as the emperor scorpions have recently been listed by CITES. I treat them here together because their housing requirements and care are similar. The most distinctive dif-

ference between Asian forest scorpions and African emperor scorpions is that the claws of the emperors are very broad and have distinctive bumps all over them. The claws of Asian forest scorpions are more slender and almost totally smooth.

Both Asian forest scorpions and African emperor scorpions exhibit primitive social behavior in the wild. They live in groups in extensive burrow systems. Because of their sociality, these scorpions can be kept together in captivity. The immatures are dependent on the mother for a much longer time than most nonsocial scorpion species. If you find yourself with a very young Asian forest scorpion or African emperor scorpion that will not eat, you can try to hand-feed it crushed food items (such as crickets) just like Mom does.

Keeping Asian forest scorpions and African emperor scorpions: Both these species will do well in a terrarium with a deep substrate to allow them to dig a burrow. You can also provide artificial burrows as for the opportunistic burrowing tarantulas. I would keep the scorpions in larger cages than for similarly sized tarantulas, as scorpions in general are more active. If you want to house a group, allow for more than one retreat as there may be a squabble between individuals in the group. If you keep individual Asian forest and African emperor scorpions in smaller containers, make

The same scorpion viewed under ultraviolet light. The fluorescence is due to the molecular structure of the cuticle; there is no apparent reason for this phenomenon.

The Emperor Scorpion (**Pandinus imperator**)
making a meal of an unfortunate gecko.

sure that it is well made. I have heard stories of
emperor scorpions unweaving wire mesh cage
tops and escaping! Yes, they have very strong
pincers. If you need to handle or transfer the
scorpion from cage to cage, you can easily pick
them up by the tail with a large forceps. Do not
do what some hurried individuals do, which is
to pick them up by the tail tip using bare fingers! Even if you secure the stinger, they can
reach up and give quite a pinch. You should
have one of the extra-large forceps on hand for
general bug wrangling in any case.

In case one of the females gives birth, leave
her alone. If the cage is crowded remove the
nonreproductive individuals. Otherwise, they
may prey on the young. Sometimes female
scorpions with young, like incubating tarantulas, turn cannibal for no readily apparent reason. Keeping them feeling safe, secure, and
well fed is your best bet. There is no reason to
have to remove the juveniles, but if you need
to, make sure they are feeding themselves first.

These scorpions like a moist environment, so
pay close attention to the water supply. The
scorpions will readily eat crickets and about
any other feeder bug. I have known people to
feed emperor scorpions young mice and rats,
but this is not necessary.

Arizona Hairy Scorpions

Arizona hairy scorpions are among the
largest scorpions in the United States. They are
native to the Sonoran Desert. They are a very
handsome pale green-yellow color. And yes,
they look hairy, particularly on the claws. They
have a heavy stinger but are not known to be

dangerously poisonous to normal, healthy
adults. They are solitary dwellers in burrows
and come to the surface at night to feed.

Keeping Arizona hairy scorpions: These
animals need a drier caging situation than
Asian forest and emperor scorpions. They will
do well in a plastic shoe box or a small terrarium with a sandy substrate and a piece of bark
to hide under. They should have a dry environment and do not need water available at all
times. I would offer it every few weeks, but
if they get the substrate in their cage wet,
change the substrate or you will have a very
unhappy scorpion until it dries. They will eat
insects of many kinds, particularly crickets.
They can go on extended fasts but as long as
they look fat, there is no cause for concern.

South African Rock Scorpions

These scorpions have the most unusual body
shape of any scorpion; they are tremendously
flattened and elongated. They are a handsome
light brown color and are fairly large, longer
than Asian forest scorpions. They are native to
rock outcrops in southern Africa where their
body shape allows them to wedge themselves
into deep cracks in the rock, safe from predation
and the burning sun. They share these habitats
with another oddly flattened animal, the

pancake tortoise. These scorpions are not currently often seen in pet shops, but are worth looking for because of their unusual appearance and gentle temperament. They have a ridiculously tiny stinger for their body size. It may be that they have been shaped by evolution to defend themselves by hiding, not stinging.

Keeping African rock scorpions: South African rock scorpions need dry conditions as do Arizona hairy scorpions. They are climbers and need a tall tank with a pile of flattened stones to climb on. They feed well on crickets and other insects.

Those Weird Spider Relatives

There are many orders in the class Arachnida—11 to 17, depending on the source. I have talked about only two of these so far: the Araneae (spiders), and Scorpiones (scorpions). I also have mentioned the mites as pests. There are three other arachnid orders worth mentioning as they are of interest to collectors: the Uropygi, whipscorpions; the Amblypygi, tailless whipscorpions; and the Solifugae, windscorpions. These three weird creatures are so strange to behold and observe feeding and moving around that it is a "close encounter of the third kind." They are so unearthly in appearance and so unlike even the relatively familiar spiders and scorpions that having one is a real treat. None of them have venom glands, which makes them less problematic to keep than many scorpions. All are restricted to warmer areas of the world.

Whipscorpions

Whipscorpions get their name from their antennalike tail (or flagellum). They also are notable for a unique chemical defense—they spray acetic acid. Their pincers have many spines on them and they are carried tucked together in front of their bodies. Their first pair of legs are modified as feelers, being long and slender. While whipscorpions are found throughout the warmer parts of the world, you are most likely to see the species found in the United States for sale. This is lucky because this whipscorpion, the giant vinegaroon (*Mastigoproctus giganteus*) is the world's largest, at over 2½ inches (approximately 6 cm) body length. They live in the southwestern United States and Florida. They dig deep burrows under stones and logs. Like scorpions, whipscorpions mate by passing a spermatophore from male to female. Unlike scorpions, whipscorpions lay eggs that they carry in a sac. The newly hatched young ride on the mother's back. The young stay with the females through several molts in the burrow.

Keeping whipscorpions: Whip-scorpions get over the acetic acid-spraying habit in captivity, which is fortunate, because they can gas themselves if they spray in an enclosed container. Whipscorpions adapt well to captivity and are best kept on a sandy substrate that is kept moist. If you do not give them a substrate deep enough for retreat construction, then you should give them a cork bark shelter to hide under during the day or they will wear themselves out trying to dig a burrow. They feed well on insects and can become so fat that they may actually eat themselves to a standstill.

Tailless Whipscorpions

Tailless whipscorpions are among the weirdest of the weird. They have a flattened body and *extremely* long legs that are several times their body length. The first pair of legs are greatly modified as sensory organs and are even longer. It is the way they move these whips around, slowly feeling for what is in their environment, that really puts them out there. Some tropical species are quite large, having a body length of about 2 inches (about 5 cm). They also have a whip span of over 1½ feet (about 50 cm). Tailless whipscorpions are among the most delicate of the arachnids. The only places I have seen tailless whipscorpions in the wild were very moist, such as in piles of rotting cardboard on the Florida Keys, and in a bat cave, a hollow tree, and a water cistern in the rain forest of French Guiana. Tailless whipscorpions are climbers, not burrowers. They are extremely fast and tricky to keep. If you are lucky enough to find one for sale (or luckier still to see one in the wild) you will need to treat it with extra care. Reproductive behavior is the same as in whipscorpions. Females carry the eggs in a sac under the abdomen, and the youngsters stay on the female's back for a brief period after hatching.

Keeping tailless whipscorpions: Tailless whipscorpions are best kept as arboreal tarantulas, with a bark chip or potting soil substrata for maintaining a higher humidity and pieces of bark to climb on. For the larger species, use one of the extratall aquaria. Rather than an open wire mesh top, I would partially mask the open mesh with plastic to restrict airflow. They need a secure climbing surface and high humidity. The bark and substrate should always be kept moist and a large water dish full of water. Even though tailless whipscorpions are from warm areas of the globe, they are nocturnal and spend their days in caves and tree hollows. They will do best at moderate temperatures, such as the lower 70s°F (20s°C) and can be killed by overly warm temperatures. They can be kept in groups if they are similar in size (otherwise, the smaller ones will be lunch). They feed well on climbing insects such as crickets. They are fast and fragile and will shed legs if you try to handle them. It is best to use a hands-off approach due to their delicate nature.

Windscorpions

Windscorpions are fast denizens of dry, warm regions of the world. In the United States they are found in the Southwest and Florida. Some of the largest are from the deserts of North Africa. Windscorpions, more than any other arachnid I have discussed, are active and aggressive predators. They have three pairs of running legs, the front pair of legs modified as feelers (like the tailless whipscorpions), the pedipalps ending in grabbing appendages that lack the grasping claws that scorpions have but have adhesive hairs. These sticky appendages pull the hapless prey into the huge chelicerae that have been modified into chopping tools. If there is a chain saw murderer analog among the Arachnida, windscorpions are it. Windscorpions either live in burrows or use retreats under stones. Males actively transfer a spermatophore to females either directly, genital orifice to genital orifice, or use the chelicerae to transfer the packet. Females lay eggs in burrows in the ground.

Keeping windscorpions: Windscorpions vary in how well they do in captivity. Most reports indicate that they live for only weeks, or at best months, in captivity. This is similar to my own experience. One reason for mortality may be that these very active critters need much

A whipscorpion or vinegaroon
(Mastigoproctus giganteus).

more space than a similarly sized scorpion or spider. There is definitely room for experimentation with windscorpions. They need a dry cage with an opportunity to burrow. Give them room, warmth, and solitude. There are indications that air movement may be important to keeping them successfully. These creatures are arachnid shrews, hungry and aggressive. I would not dream of handling them. They are best transferred between cages using the hands-off method. Remember, they are very fast. They will eat a wide variety of insects and small vertebrates. Feed them a lot, much more than a scorpion of similar size.

A pair of Tanzanian tailless whipscorpions. Note the white spermatophore on the bark between them.

INFORMATION

Following is a brief list of societies and sources of information for tarantula and arachnid care. In addition, there are multiple sites on the World Wide Web as well as computer bulletin boards devoted to arachnids. As these are likely to change frequently, I will leave it up to the reader to locate current sites and addresses.

Societies

The American Tarantula Society
P.O. Box 756
Carlsbad, NM 88221

The British Tarantula Society
81 Phillimore Place
Radlett, Hertfordshire, WD7 8NJ
England

American Arachnological Society
American Museum of Natural History
Central Park West at 79th Street
New York, NY 10024

British Arachnological Society
71 Havant Road
Walthamstow, London E17 3JE
England

Sources for Tarantulas

Many vendors offer tarantulas for sale. I list three sources for tarantulas that I have worked with and have had excellent dealings with over the years. All have web sites you can find using any search engine.

Arachnocentric
1107 W. Oak St.
West Frankfort, IL 62896
Phone (618) 932-3467
Fax (618) 932-6282
Arachnocentric specializes in captive-bred tarantula spiderlings.

Glades Herp
5207 Palm Beach Blvd.
Ft. Myers, FL 33905
Phone (941) 693-1077
Fax (941) 693-1901
Glades Herp has a diverse species listing, and often has unusual tarantulas for sale.

West Coast Zoological
P.O. Box 16840
Plantation, FL 33318
Phone (954) 327-8504
Fax (954) 327-8264
West Coast Zoological is a world-wide importer that has good prices on wild-caught spiders.

Sources for Supplies or Feeder Insects

Carolina Biological Supply Co.
2700 York Road
Burlington, NC 27215
(800) 334-5551
Carolina sells fruit flies and rearing media.

Ward's Natural Science
P.O. Box 92912
Rochester, NY 14692-9012
(800) 962-2660
Ward's sells fruit flies, rearing media and window cages (for web spiders).

BioQuip Products
17803 LaSalle Avenue
Gardena, CA 90248
(310) 324-0620
BioQuip sells insect collecting equipment, including sweep nets and black lights, insect cages, and books.

Top Hat Cricket Farm, Inc.
1919 Forest Drive
Kalamazoo, MI 49002
(800) 638-2555

Fluker Farms
P.O. Box 378
Baton Rouge, LA 70821
(800) 735-8537

Grubco
P.O. Box 15001
Hamilton, OH 45015
(800) 222-3563

I N D E X

African emperor scorpion, 104–105
African redrump tarantula, 48
Anatomy, 6–8, 10
Andean stripeleg tarantula, 63–65
Antilles pinktoe tarantula, 70
Arizona hairy scorpion, 105
Asian chevron tarantula, 46, 48
Asian forest scorpion, 104–105

Bedding, 23–25, 86
Behavior, 26–27
Bite, 15
Black widow, 98–100
Bolivian steelyblue tarantula, 61–62
Book lungs, 8, 11
Brazilian salmon tarantula, 56–57, 60
Brazilian whiteknee tarantula, 62, 64
Breeding:
  considerations for, 27
  description of, 78–79
  pair for, 73–76
  signals, 77–78
Burrowers:
  obligate, 14, 28–29
  opportunistic, 14, 28
Buying, 17–20

Cage. See also Housing
  bedding, 23–25, 86
  considerations for, 20–21
  humidity in, 21–22
  substrates, 22–25
Cameroon red tarantula, 27, 48–50
Cannibalism, 73, 85
Characteristics, 5
Chilean common tarantula, 13, 26, 58, 60
Cobalt blue tarantula, 45–46
Colombian giant tarantula, 60–61
Colombian lesserblack tarantula, 58
Costa Rican tigerrump tarantula, 13
Costa Rican zebra tarantula, 62–63, 76

Crickets, 90
Curlyhair tarantula, 69
Curvedhorn tarantula, 48

Defense, 15
Diet, 34–36
Digestion, 10

Earthworms, 93
Ecuadorian brownvelvet tarantula, 60
Eggs:
  artificial incubation of, 82–83
  eating of, 92
  laying of, 79, 81–82
Equipment, 19

False Death's Head cockroach, 93
Fangs, 11
Feeding:
  schedule for, 35–36
  spiderlings, 87
Flour beetles, 92
Foldingdoor spiders, 97–98
Food:
  amount of, 35–36
  commercial sources, 89–93
  prey, 34–35
Fruit flies, 90–91
Fungal infections, 95
Fungus gnats, 33–34

Giant crab spiders, 102
Goliath birdeater tarantula, 15, 54–57
Greenbottle blue tarantula, 29, 61–62

Habitat, 5–6, 14
Hairs, urticating, 15, 20
Haitian brown tarantula, 57–58, 60
Handling, 38–39
History, 6
Housing. See also Cage
  for arboreals, 31
  considerations for, 20–21
  dangers associated with, 31
  for obligate burrowers, 28–29
  for opportunistic burrowers, 28
  for spiderlings, 86

utilitarian, 25, 27
  vivaria, 27–28
Humidity, 19, 21–22
Hybridizing, 74–75

Illness, 94–95
Indian ornamental tarantula, 51–52, 56

Java yellowknee tarantula, 54, 56

King baboon tarantula, 50, 52

Laws, 59
Leg loss, 94–95
Longevity, 10–11

Maggots, 33
Mail-order buying, 18
Mealworms, 91–92
Mexican blond tarantula, 64–67, 80
Mexican redknee tarantula, 67–68
Mexican redleg tarantula, 68, 80
Mexican redrump tarantula, 68–69
Mites, 31–33
Molting, 36–37, 95
Mombassa golden starburst tarantula, 46–47
Myiasis, 20

Obligate burrowers, 14, 28–29
Opportunistic burrowers, 14, 28
Orange treespider tarantula, 71
Orbweavers, 100–102

Panama blond tarantula, 16
Peruvian blond tarantula, 13
Pinktoe tarantula, 12, 69–70
Pompillid wasp, 12, 14
Purseweb spiders, 97–98

Red featherleg tarantula, 51, 53
Regulatory agencies, 59
Reproductive organs, 76–77

Reputation, 6–7
Respiratory organs, 11

Scorpions, 102–106
Scuttle flies, 33
Sex, 9
Shedding. See Molting
Shipping, 20, 75
Silk, 8
Skeleton tarantula, 12–13, 71
Soil substrate, 22–23
South African rock scorpion, 105–106
Sphagnum moss, 24
Spiderlings:
  description of, 18, 83
  feeding of, 87
  housing of, 86
  separating of, 85–86
Sri Lankan ornamental tarantula, 51–52
Straighthorned tarantula, 47–49
Substrates:
  making of, 23–24
  soil, 22–23
Superworms, 93
Systematics, 41–45

Tanzania dwarf tarantula, 45
Temperature, 22, 87
Thailand black tarantula, 46
Thailand zebra tarantula, 46, 48
Togo starburst tarantula, 50–51, 53
Trapdoor spiders, 97–98
Trinidad chevron tarantula, 52–54
Trinidad mahogany tarantula, 70–71
Trinidad olive tarantula, 63–64, 80

Usambara orange tarantula, 49

Venom, 15
Vermiculite, 24
Vivarium, 27–30

Wandering spiders, 102
Whipscorpions, 106–107
Widow spiders, 98–100
Windscorpions, 107–108

About the Author

Sam Marshall has kept and studied tarantulas since 1974, when he caught his first tarantula in Arizona. Since then he has traveled to South America, Australia, and the Caribbean in search of tarantulas. He has earned both Master's and Doctoral degrees studying spiders, and has performed research on tarantulas in the field and lab, studying their systematics, behavior and ecology. The results of his work has been published in both popular and scientific venues. Sam is currently the director of Hiram College's J. H. Barrow Field Station in northeast Ohio, where he conducts research on tarantulas and wolf spiders with Hiram College students.

Photo Credits

All photos by Samuel D. Marshall except page 56 (bottom left) by Rick C. West.

Important Note

The subject of this book is the keeping and care of a venomous animal. Tarantula and scorpion keepers should be aware that any bite or sting, even one where the spider or scorpion is not particularly toxic, should be considered serious and may have harmful consequences. See a physician immediately after any bite or sting. Some species have urticating hairs that they shed in defense (see page 15). Such hairs can irritate the skin or throat if inhaled. Always guard against inhaling these hairs or having them come in contact with the skin. If there is contact, wash hands thoroughly and seek a physician's care immediately if a persistent rash or inflammation occurs.

Keeping tarantulas and scorpions requires great care and responsibility. Carelessness can lead to serious consequences. Children should always be supervised when observing your spider or scorpion, and individuals with small children are advised not to keep these animals.

Some vivarium plants may be harmful to the skin or mucous membranes of human beings. If you notice any signs of irritation, wash the area thoroughly. See your physician if the condition persists.

All inquiries should be addressed to:
Barron's Educational Series, Inc.
250 Wireless Boulevard
Hauppauge, NY 11788
http://www.barronseduc.com

International Standard Book No. 0-7641-1463-8

Library of Congress Catalog Card No. 00-058576

Library of Congress Cataloging-in-Publication Data
Marshall, Samuel D.
    Tarantulas and other arachnids : everything about purchase, housing, care, nutrition, and health care / Samuel D. Marshall ; illustrations by Laura Barghusen.
        p.   cm.
    Includes bibliographical references (p.   ).
    ISBN 0-7641-1463-8
    1. Tarantulas as pets. 2. Tarantulas. 3. Arachnida.
I. Title.
SF429.T37 M37   2001
639'.7—dc21   00-058576

Printed in Hong Kong

9 8 7 6 5 4 3 2 1